Charles Simic

in conversation with

Michael Hulse

Charles Simic

in conversation with

Michael Hulse

BETWEEN THE LINES **BTL** BETWEEN THE LINES

First published in 2002 by

BTL
BETWEEN THE LINES BTL BETWEEN THE LINES

9 Woodstock Road
London N4 3ET
UK

T : +44 (0)20 8374 5526   F : +44 (0)20 8374 5736   E-mail : btluk@aol.com
Website: http://www.interviews-with-poets.com

© Questions: Michael Hulse
© Answers: Charles Simic

© Photograph of Charles Simic: Philip Simic

© 'Independence Day', 'The Secret Doctrine', 'Nearest Nameless', 'Empty Barbershop':
Charles Simic

©Artwork on back cover: Philip Hoy

© Editorial Matter: Between The Lines

The right of Michael Hulse to be identified as the author of this work
has been asserted by him in accordance with
the Copyright, Designs and Patents Act of 1988

A CIP catalogue record for this book is available from the British Library

ISBN 1-903291-03-8

Design and typography: Philip Hoy

Printed and bound by George Over Limited
Somers Road, Rugby CV22 7DH

BETWEEN THE LINES **BTL** BETWEEN THE LINES

BTL publishes unusually wide-ranging and unusually deep-going interviews with some of today's most accomplished poets.

Some would deny that any useful purpose is served by putting to a writer questions which are not answered by his or her books. For them, what Yeats called "the bundle of accident and incoherence that sits down to breakfast" is best left alone, not asked to interrupt its cornflakes, or to set aside its morning paper, while someone with a tape recorder inquires about its life, habits and attitudes.

If we do not share this view, it is not because we endorse Sainte-Beuve's dictum, *tel arbre, tel fruit* — *as the tree, so the fruit* — but because we understand what Geoffrey Braithwaite was getting at when the author of *Flaubert's Parrot* had him say:

> But if you love a writer, if you depend upon the drip-feed
> of his intelligence, if you want to pursue him and find
> him – despite edicts to the contrary – then it's impossible
> to know too much.

The first ten volumes, featuring W.D. Snodgrass, Michael Hamburger, Anthony Thwaite, Anthony Hecht, Donald Hall, Thom Gunn, Richard Wilbur, Seamus Heaney, Donald Justice and Ian Hamilton, respectively, are already available; others now being prepared will feature Peter Dale, John Ashbery, Paul Muldoon, and Peter Porter (Further details are given overleaf.)

As well as the interview, each volume contains a sketch of the poet's life and career, a comprehensive bibliography, archival information, and a representative selection of quotations from the poet's critics and reviewers. More recent volumes also contain uncollected poems. It is hoped that the results will be of interest to the lay reader and specialist alike.

— OTHER VOLUMES FROM BTL —

W.D. SNODGRASS
in conversation with
Philip Hoy

MICHAEL HAMBURGER
in conversation with
Peter Dale

ANTHONY THWAITE
in conversation with
Peter Dale and Ian Hamilton

ANTHONY HECHT
in conversation with
Philip Hoy

DONALD HALL
in conversation with
Ian Hamilton

THOM GUNN
in conversation with
James Campbell

RICHARD WILBUR
in conversation with
Peter Dale

SEAMUS HEANEY
in conversation with
Karl Miller

DONALD JUSTICE
in conversation with
Philip Hoy

IAN HAMILTON
in conversation with
Dan Jacobson

— FORTHCOMING —

PETER DALE
in conversation with
William Bedford

PAUL MULDOON
in conversation with
Lavinia Greenlaw

JOHN ASHBERY
in conversation with
Mark Ford

PETER PORTER
in conversation with
John Kinsella

CONTENTS

ACKNOWLEDGEMENTS

The editors would like to thank Philip Simic for allowing them to use the photograph shown on the front cover and on page 10. They would also like to thank William S. Brockman (Pennsylvania State University Library), James McKinley and Angela Elam (New Letters on the Air, University of Missouri), and the staff of the Rare Book & Special Collections Library at the University of Illinois at Urbana-Champaign for having supplied them with information or material necessary for completion of the bibliography and the critical quotes section appearing at the end of this book.

Charles Simic

Photograph courtesy of
Philip Simic

A Note on Charles Simic

Charles Simic was born in Belgrade, Yugoslavia, on May 9th 1938, the first son of George and Helen (Matijevic) Simic.

As a boy, Simic received what he quotes Jan Kott as calling "a typical East European education" – an education, that's to say, in which "Hitler and Stalin taught us the basics." What the basics involved is well described in the poet's recently published memoir, *A Fly in the Soup*, where, amongst other things, he tells us that "[b]y the time my brother was born, and he and my mother had come home from the clinic, I was in the business of selling gunpowder. Many of us kids had stashes of ammunition, which we collected during the street fighting."

Towards the end of the war, Simic's father fled the country, and it was to be ten years before the family would see him again. He had made his way to America, where pre war employment by an American company (he was an engineer) had given him numerous contacts. However, his wife and children were unable to follow until 1954, the Communist authorities having denied them a passport until 1953, and the US immigration authorities having taken another year or so to process their visa application.

After a year in New York, the family moved to Chicago, where Simic attended Oak Park High School, an earlier alumnus of which had been Ernest Hemingway. He graduated in 1956, but instead of going to college, like most of his peers – his parents had very little in the way of savings, but in any case seem not to have given any thought to the possibility – he found work, first as an office boy, and later as a proof-reader, at the Chicago *Sun Times.*

It was during this period that Simic started to write poetry. His poetic enthusiasms were various – one month a disciple of Hart Crane, the next a devotee of Walt Whitman – yet this was no mere dalliance: "I'd work at it all night, go to work half-asleep, and then drag myself to night classes."

In 1958, Simic left Chicago and went back to New York. There he continued to work by day – as parcel-packer, shirt salesman, house painter, book-seller, payroll clerk – and to study by night. He also continued to write, and after a year or more saw his first poems in print, in the Winter 1959 issue of the *Chicago Review.*

Drafted into the army in 1961, Simic spent most of his two years' service in Germany and France, working as a military policeman. From a literary historian's point of view, probably the most noteworthy thing about Simic's time in the army is that it led him to a radical reappraisal of the sort of poetry he'd been writing. Indeed, so radical was the reappraisal that he ended up destroying everything he'd written, later describing it as "no more than literary vomit".

After discharge from the army, Simic returned to the life he'd been leading in New York. In 1964, he married Helen Dubin, a fashion designer, and in 1967 he obtained his BA from New York University. A year later his first collection of poems was released by the San Francisco publisher, Kayak. The book was reviewed at some length by William Matthews, who, although he had plenty of criticisms to make, recognized the young poet's potential: "I found *What the Grass Says* exciting ... What I like in Simic's poems ... is his seriousness ... [and] I am impatient to read more ..."

In 1966, Simic went to work as an editorial assistant for the photography magazine, *Aperture*, a job he held until 1969, the year of his second collection, *Somewhere Among Us a Stone Is Taking Notes*, also published by Kayak. Diane Wakoski's review of this book opened with the memorable words: "I have not yet decided whether Charles Simic is America's greatest living Surrealist poet, a children's writer, a religious writer, or simple-minded." In fact, and as the rest of her review made clear, Wakoski was a lot closer to thinking Simic the country's greatest living Surrealist than to thinking him simple-minded. Simic was just thirty-one, but was already gathering a following.

The year after *Somewhere Among Us a Stone Is Taking Notes* was published, Simic was offered a teaching position in California State College, Hayward, and he remained there until 1973, when he was offered an associate professorship at the University of New Hampshire. He has remained at UNH to this day, though long since promoted to the position of full professor.

In the thirty-six years since his first collection appeared, Simic has published more than sixty books, amongst them *Charon's Cosmology* (1977), which was nominated for a National Book Award, *Classic Ballroom Dances* (1980), which won the University of Chicago's Harriet Monroe Award and the Poetry Society of America's di Castagnola Award, *The World Doesn't End: Prose Poems* (1990), which won the Pulitzer Prize for Poetry (a prize for which he had been nominated on two previous occasions, in 1986 and 1987), *Walking the Black Cat* (1996), which was a finalist for the National Book Award, and *Jackstraws* (1999), which was nominated a Notable Book of the Year by the *New York Times*. Simic has also been honoured with two PEN Awards for his distinguished work as a translator (1970, 1980), a Guggenheim Fellowship (1972), two National Endowment for the Arts Fellowships (1974, 1979), the American Academy of Poets' Edgar Allan Poe Award (1975), the American Academy Award (1976), a Fulbright Fellowship (1982), an Ingram Merrill Fellowship (1983), a MacArthur Fellowship (1984), an Academy of American Poets' Fellowship (1998), and the University of New Hampshire's Lindberg Award "for his achievements as both an outstanding scholar and teacher in the College of Liberal Arts" (2002). In 2000, he was appointed a Chancellor of the Academy of American Poets, and a little earlier this year he was also elected a Fellow of the American Academy of Arts and Sciences.

Simic and his wife – who have a son and daughter – live in Strafford, New Hampshire.

A Note on Michael Hulse

Michael Hulse was born in Stoke-on-Trent, Staffordshire in 1955, and educated locally (1966-1971) and at the University of St Andrews (1973-1977), where he took an MA in German. From the late Seventies until very recently, he lived in Germany, working as a university lecturer, and as an editor, reviewer, translator and publisher.

Hulse's poetry collections include *Knowing and Forgetting* (Secker and Warburg, London, 1981), *Propaganda* (Secker and Warburg, London 1985), and *Eating Strawberries in the Necropolis* (Collins Harvill, London, 1991). A new collection, *Empires and Holy Lands: Poems 1976-2000,* appeared from Salt Publishing (Cambridge) earlier this year.

Amongst the fifty or more books Hulse has translated into English are J.W. Goethe's *Sorrows of Young Werther* (Penguin, London, 1989), Jakob Wassermann's *Caspar Hauser* (Penguin, London, 1992), Botho Strauss's *Tumult* (Carcanet, Manchester/New York, 1984), and W.G. Sebald's *The Emigrants* (Harvill, London/New Directions, New York, 1996), *The Rings of Saturn* (Harvill, London/New Directions, New York, 1998) and *Vertigo* (Harvill, London/New Directions, New York, 1999).

Hulse is editorial director of Leviathan Press and editor of *Leviathan Quarterly*. This autumn, he returned to live in England, where he has joined the Writing Programme at the University of Warwick.

THE CONVERSATION

What follows is an edited version of written exchanges that took place between April and December of 2001.

It occurs to me time and again, when I read your poems, essays, notes or aphorisms, that they outdistance commentary. That is, they already contain within them, completely and perfectly, the terms by which they might be described, analysed or criticised. To write the definitive critical account of Charles Simic's work, one would have to be another Pierre Menard and write once again, word for word, the poetry and prose of Charles Simic. Is this interview therefore pointless?

Every time one opens one's mouth there is a chance that one may say something new. Besides, I certainly don't have the impression that I have figured everything out for myself. *Au contraire*, as the Frenchies say: I'm still in the dark about a lot of things.

We are conducting this interview by e-mail, and I am writing this next question without knowing your reply to the first. If your answer amounted to "yes", the reader may as well stop here. If it amounted to "no", an interesting matter arises: for a sensibility alive at pretty full stretch, what is the source of the faith that something worthwhile can be said the next time the "maternal silence" is broken?

There's a paradox here. On the one hand, we are all limited, have a few pet notions we return to again and again, and on the other hand, we live our lives and things happen to us – nice things and not-so-nice things – so one is bound to have a new thought once in a while.

To begin at the beginning, then, with the language out of which poetry is made: the more I think of it, the more striking it appears that in joining the company of Conrad, Nabokov and other writers who have achieved pre-eminence in a language they were not born to, you have done so not in the medium of prose but in that of poetry. This is more than a Campion or Milton writing in Latin, or a Rilke venturing into French or Russian: this is total identification and transformation, a phenomenon virtually unknown among poets. You've described your learning of English after

17

you left Belgrade, first in Paris (1953-54) and then in New York; your first reading of literature in English; and your first attempts to write poetry, in Chicago in 1956, apparently in English already. Did you never write poetry in the language of your childhood?

I never did. Back in 1970, when they were about to publish a selection of my poems in Belgrade, the editors asked me to translate one poem myself into Serbian. I said sure, I'd be delighted. Then, to my surprise, I found that I could not. I knew all the words, of course, but had lost the feel for what they do to the native speaker. In English I was already playing with the connotations of words and idioms, while I seemed to have lost that ability in Serbian. It was kind of disconcerting. English had been the language I had used almost exclusively on a daily basis for many years, and those were the unforeseen consequences.

Despite what some poets have claimed, about how they only write for themselves, the truth is that one wants one's poems read. In my case, it was usually some girl I was falling in love with or a friend interested in literature, so I had to write in a language they would understand, and that was English. This did not strike me as odd at the time. Only much later was I told that it was.

Were you conscious, as you produced the large number of poems in your late teens and early twenties which you "had the pleasure of destroying" in 1962, of any interference from the other language you had had? Did a sense of that earlier language dog your composition, influence for better or worse your choice of words, syntax, images?

I wrote my first poems in English in 1955, and for the next few years I would hear in my head simultaneously both the English and the Serbian word, but at some point, without my being aware of it, that ended. The poems I threw away struck me as shamelessly derivative and badly written. The few that I still have left from that period, like the ones published in the winter issue of the *Chicago Review* in 1959, are not so hot either.

Writing poetry is many things, but most of all it is an obsession with language. Words make love to our imagination and vice versa. It would be unlikely to be smitten with a phrase in Serbian and then turn around and write a poem in English.

Reading your autobiographical writings, it's impossible to tell whether or when the language spoken at home, between yourself and your parents, changed. From your mother's getting in touch with Serbians she knew on arrival in Oak Park, and your father's catching you up on family history in Serbia and elsewhere, I've assumed the language spoken at home remained Serbo-Croat. Can you point to a time when you first felt you inhabited English fully and comfortably?

It would have to be when I was in the Army in 1961-63. I was a military policeman, an occupation in which one has to appear super-confident, especially when one is arresting a drunk wielding a broken beer bottle in a bar. After two years of that I felt at home in the language.

What made all the difference in my case, when it came to speaking English, is that I left home when I was eighteen. I can't believe I did it, but I packed up and left to escape my parents' endless bickering. My brother, who is seven years younger than me, and so was eleven at that time, became fluent in English very quickly and refused to speak Serbian at home. Afterwards when I saw them, I spoke Serbian with my mother and a mixture of English and Serbian with my father. The old man was an Anglophile, wore tweeds, smoked a pipe, had the London *Times* or *New Statesman* sticking out of his pocket, and had been an ardent fan of Aston Villa since the Twenties, so naturally we spoke plenty of English.

Homer and Virgil aside, the prose writers and poets you mention by name amongst your wide reading in the period up to 1959, when the Chicago Review *published your poems for the first time, were all Anglophone: Twain, Hemingway and Joyce, Whitman and Crane, Pound and Stevens, Lowell and Jarrell. And yet you've written: "Every great lyric poem recapitulates the whole history of inspired listening to the mother tongue." What of your own mother tongue? Which poets of Yugoslavia were important to you in the years before the mid-Sixties when you first read and translated Lalic?*

In the fall of 1963, in the New York Public Library, I discovered a large collection of Yugoslav poetry and I made my first translations of Popa and Lalic. There's no question they influenced me. Before that time, I was not familiar with modern Yugoslav poetry, but I knew and loved the folk poetry, both epic and lyric, which I read as a small child in Yugoslavia. My father had several large collections of them in his library and I kept going back to them. The lyric poems, a few of which I translated, made a great impact on me. It's the first poetry that brought tears to my eyes. I guess that must mean something.

Can you comment more fully on the importance of Vasko Popa for you?

I have a sense of the impact he made on you in the early Sixties surviving for a very long time: for instance, the six-legged dog in 'Country Fair' reminds me of the eight-legged horse you drew attention to in introducing your translated selection of Popa's poems.

Except his horse was a mythical being and my dog was a real New England mutt. Popa was an influence, both as a poet and as a thinker. He had carefully thought through the various implications of Surrealist practice and other poetic movements since the Symbolists and his reflections made a great deal of sense to me, even as I grew more and more aware that I'm a very different poet from him. Still, his notion that one had to make one's way critically among the many aesthetic and philosophical ideas made a big impact on me. He made poetry an intellectual adventure in addition to everything else it is. The only thing I couldn't understand is that he continued to be a Communist, since he certainly was not a materialist and in fact had great admiration for the art and esoteric literature of the Eastern Orthodox Church.

He was also great company, always ready for an endless conversation on any subject. In that respect he was like my father. They met in New York when Popa was in the United States for an extended stay and they got along well. We'd all meet in a Greek restaurant on Eighth Avenue, eat lunch and spend the rest of the afternoon at the same table drinking wine and talking about anything from mysticism to women. One time, we were so absorbed in what we were talking about we didn't notice the dinner guests were beginning to arrive. So what did we do when we did eventually notice? We ordered dinner, of course.

In the notebook extracts gathered in The Unemployed Fortune-Teller, *and again in your* LRB *review of his* Collected Poems, *you describe Popa giving a detailed account of the poems he meant to write, and add that you subsequently saw those poems coming into print over the years. It's a practice radically different from anything you've suggested your own is. How suspect, or how appealing, do you find an approach to poetry that apparently excludes almost entirely the experience of chance, caprice, serendipity, everything that has been gathered conventionally under that label of convenience, "inspiration"?*

I never knew anyone who wrote the way Popa did. There are other poets who give the impression that they know pretty much what they are going to say before they start, but Popa calculated what he would write years before he put down any words on the page. Still, he left room for chance.

He had the idea of what the whole was going to be about, and even the titles of individual poems, but not the imagery and play of metaphors. He was like the artist Joseph Cornell, who would first find a box, give it a title, and then spend years finding various objects to put in it. They both believed in a strict form within which chance rules. All poets work like that to a degree. Popa was just an extreme case.

Thinking of Vasko Popa's experiences in life, as well as of his poetry, it occurs to me that he united within himself much that was found in various eastern European poets in the post-Second World War decades: Marxist convictions, time in a concentration camp, serious philosophical interests, variance with the Communist Party of which he was a member. Is there not a sense in which your own eastern European generation, born when Popa's was in its mid-teens, looks to the credentials of the elders with something akin to envy?

I can't speak for the others, but personally all that didn't mean anything to me. My intellectual life began long after I left Europe. Marxism, the rudiments of which I was taught in school in Yugoslavia, I thought was a joke, and the same goes for Communism. When I met Popa and that generation of poets and intellectuals, I found their world constricted. There were so many things they did not dare say or think. It was depressing. One had to tiptoe around certain issues, and that certainly was not my habit even then. One of my dearest and oldest friends, Ivan Lalic, was cautious to the very end of his life. He'd either remain silent or laugh while I railed against Serbian nationalism. So, while I admired them as poets and liked them as people, they could not be role models. Frankly, I thought they lived cowardly lives.

Writing on Popa's Collected Poems in 1999, you described him as "capable of a verbal dazzle that makes him sound at times like Paul Muldoon". Could you elaborate on the points of resemblance?

That doesn't come through in translation. Poetry that relies so much on the genius of a particular language is hard to translate. Popa tried to use the full resources of the Serbian literary and spoken idiom. Muldoon operates like that, too, within a very different literary tradition, of course. I cannot imagine him being translated with any kind of success. I spoke earlier of "chance" in connection with Popa. What he had in mind by that is that moment when the native idiom of the poet takes over and begins to write the poem, when the words begin to make love on the page.

21

You've recalled a French teacher giving you contemporary French poetry, and going to the Newberry Library in Chicago to read the French Surrealists. In the early days you considered yourself a Surrealist. What else did you take from French poetry as you found your own feet?

As Octavio Paz used to say, for a long time modern poetry and modern painting meant Paris. Sure, there was Eliot and a few others elsewhere, but the French were what everyone was interested in, from Peking to Patagonia. I read and reread endlessly all the classics of the avant-garde, from Ducasse to the Surrealists. That was the curriculum if one wanted to be hip, and I certainly wanted to be.

Villon, Baudelaire, Rimbaud, Apollinaire and Desnos were my heroes. What then appealed to me was their irreverence. I grew up in post-war Belgrade listening to racy street talk. I was a punk myself, a school dropout and, later, a displaced person. I needed to blaspheme, to say no to everything. I wanted my images to be extreme, shocking, and mad. I also liked the music of French verse. In school in Paris they made us memorise poems. I loved saying "Dictes moy ou, n'en quel pays / Est Flora la belle Rommaine"... or "Sois sage, ô ma Douleur, et tiens-toi plus tranquille..." I still do.

You've described the painting you did as a young man as coming out of abstract expressionism, and showing some taste if no great talent. The point at which you gave up painting seems to have followed not only your first magazine publications as a poet but also that moment in the army in 1962 when you threw out all your poetry to date and went on, I imagine, with a changed, perhaps matured, sense of purpose. Is it right to think that your abandonment of painting was partly influenced by the realisation that it was in poetry that you were likelier to find a real gift and to say something of your own?

Well, it wasn't so clear-cut. It's not like I had one great moment of realisation. I first published poems in 1959 and didn't stop painting entirely till 1965-66. When it comes to fantasy life, being a painter has much more to offer than being a poet. One has a studio, wears paint-splattered clothes, hangs out in bars older painters frequent, and has plenty of good-looking chicks. As a poet, I knew I would have to work on some crummy nine-to-five job, send poems to magazines, and have them accepted occasionally so I could show them to a couple of equally obscure poet friends. That's more or less what happened.

I didn't have enough ability as a painter to go on, nor did I believe that

I had a great talent as a poet. It came down to what would hurt more if I gave it up: painting or poetry? Still, I met a couple of people I used to know in those days, who surprised the hell out of me by saying that they liked my paintings better than my poems.

There's a noticeable painterly quality in some of your earlier work. The very title of your collection Return to a Place Lit by a Glass of Milk *has a feel of Magritte to it, while Chagall comes very strongly to mind when I read 'Tapestry'. In fact 'Tapestry' seems very much a key early poem: it has a faux naïf busy, bustling quality, it is mysterious and primitive and folk-like, it transcends the real without buying into the full Surreal package, it suggests myth and something larger than myth without losing sight of the everyday, and it does it all in very simple terms. Would you care to comment on the poem?*

You are right. I wanted some of those poems to have a feel of primitive paintings. I never particularly cared for tapestries as art, except for the way in which all the elements of the narrative are placed side by side. Juxtaposition of unlikely things, a form of metaphysical blaspheming, where one is bound to find an angel next to a pig, is what I have always liked to see. My vision is comic, and comedy thrives on combining seemingly incompatible elements. I can't remember exactly the circumstances of writing that poem, which I did thirty-five years ago, but it was done in that spirit. After years of painting and looking at art, the visual elements continue to be important in my poetry. When I was younger, I saw more than I heard. I mean, images came first and then ideas and the music words make. Now it's almost the reverse.

Your description of "the crowded canvasses of primitive painters" in The Uncertain Certainty *is extremely revealing of a fundamental in your own aesthetics. "I understand that need to put everything in," you write, "humans, domestic animals, beasts of the forest, angels, machines. Everything in the world is going on at the same time and deserves to be included." When you go on to say that the "list" poem is "the poetic equivalent of quilt-making", and that the patches are cut "into signs and symbols of one's own cosmology", we're plainly back with 'Tapestry', but what I want to ask you about now is the emphasis on the simultaneity of things happening. You've drawn attention more than once to the notorious difficulty of rendering the synchronicity of various experiences in the linear, sequential form a poem necessarily takes as language moves forward through time. Can you comment on ways that have been attempted to overcome this difficulty, in your own poetry and that of others, and say whether you think a solution to the problem is at all possible?*

I don't know if there's a solution, but that's the crux of my problem. How to create a visual and metaphysical three-ring circus for the reader with new images and metaphors popping up all over the place. It makes me try to create something the poem is basically incapable of becoming. Of course, one is always straining against limits in poetry, coming up against paradoxes. For instance, writing, one places words in sequential order and the poem moves in time. But linear time is not what one is after. Every poem dreams of being a circle where the moment one finishes reading it, one wants to go back to the beginning and read it again. The poem both moves in time and tries to defeat time. Images, metaphors and words with their multiple meanings conspire to trap the imagination of the reader in place. Once the reader begins to intuit all these inner relationships, there's no end to the poem. A great poem, as we know, is inexhaustible to the imagination and the intellect. It has transcended time; it lives in a world in which past, present and future co-exist. I can't draw you a map of how to get there, but I know there's such a place.

It strikes me that, aside from the 1984 interview with Sherod Santos that's reprinted in The Uncertain Certainty, *in which you spoke of Mondrian, Pollock, Rothko, de Kooning, Guston and Frankenthaler in varying degrees of (dis)approbation (which I imagine may well have changed again meanwhile), and an appearance by the Douanier Rousseau in a poem in* Unending Blues, *the references to painting in your work aren't in fact ever to anything at all modern. I find Bosch ('Brooms'), Dürer ('Travelling Slaughterhouse'), Velázquez ('Evening Visitor'), Titian (the* Venus of Urbino, *I take it, in 'Men Deified Because of Their Cruelty'), as well as the "primitive painters" you admire generically in* The Uncertain Certainty *and the unidentified artist of a 'Medieval Miniature' in* Jackstraws. *The bottom line, if I place these references and their contexts alongside what appear to be your main concerns and interests generally, is that you respond most to those painters who capture vividly the bustling fullness of life, or its mad violence and menace, or the sexiness of women, but you can't be bothered too much with the merely intellectual satisfactions that many 20th century artists offer. Does this correctly describe your feelings?*

The abstract artists you mention were my gods until the day I realised the poverty of their aesthetics. It was like a composer deciding that only three notes on the piano are authentic and he is going to make music now with only these three notes. Reductionist theories along the lines of *less is more and next to nothing is even better* appealed to me in my youth. It's the view that reality is of no interest to a true artist and only certain formal considerations are worth bothering about. How stupid can you get? Still, the walls of my house are covered with abstract art, paintings I have not wearied of looking at for many years. So, I guess, when it comes to the arts, it is dangerous to generalise.

Tell me about the jazz that meant the most to you when you were buying those records as a young man. That same decade of the Fifties saw the rise of rock and roll: did it mean anything to you?

My brother listened to rock and roll. I didn't mind it, but after Charlie Parker and Lester Young, rock was kids' stuff. I have the temperament of a stamp collector. Once I heard jazz and loved it, I wanted to hear every record ever made, going back to King Oliver. I had no money to buy records then, but I had a radio and later I went to the clubs. I may have called myself a Surrealist in those days, but in truth Thelonius Monk issued my poetic license rather than André Breton. When I read about the stunts Dadaists and Surrealists used to pull, back in the Twenties, they struck me as pretty mild stuff compared to what went on in dives in New York where they played jazz. Some pop tune restructured and reinvented, until it was a work of great beauty, seemed to me the right way to proceed in the arts: find something new and original in the same old thing you hear every day ... Isn't that what poetry does, too? Plus, these musicians were real characters. Their message was: "Cultivate your madness, boy. Forget about making it in the so-called 'real world'. Raise hell every chance you get and prepare yourself for a life at the margins of society."

Jazz aside, you made an extraordinary statement about the blues in the same 1984 interview with Sherod Santos that recorded your views on modern painters. The blues, you said, "taught me a number of things. How to tell a story quickly, economically. The value of gaps, ellipses, and most importantly, the virtues of simplicity and accessibility." Now those are not merely features of your poetic technique, they are its essentials. Do you stand by this statement that it was the blues (as opposed to any of the other arts that could have taught you the same things) that gave you this understanding? If so, could you possibly elaborate, even give examples, or suggest how your temperament came to acquire this technical equipment from the blues rather than (say) from the stories of Kafka or the drawings of Goya?

I realise most people have no idea what I'm talking about for the simple reason that they haven't listened to as much blues as I have and don't have the slightest inkling of the poetry it contains. Here's Blind Lemon Jefferson from a record made in April, 1927:

> Standin' here wonderin' will a matchbox hold my clothes
> I was settin' here wonderin' will a matchbox hold my clothes
> I ain't got so many matches but I got so far to go

Even without the singer's voice, his guitar and the melody, this is pretty suggestive, I'd say. It reminded me – and I could quote hundreds of examples – how little one needs to say in order to mean so much.

The genius of the blues is that it is able to get at the heart of our human predicament. Love, betrayal, poverty, regret, injustice, illness, sex, death and a few other things – that's what it comes down to. Al Capone is reputed to have said that he preferred jazz to opera because there isn't all that snivelling in it. Blues is the poetry of tough guys and pissed-off women. Here's Roosevelt Sykes in 1931, singing and accompanying himself on the piano:

> I said, good morning Mr Pawnshop
> As I walked in his door.
> I said, I feel bad this morning
> And I really want my 44.
>
> Well, I was at a party last night.
> I was there till about half past two,
> I'm going back out there tonight
> I might have some shooting to do.
>
> Now the policemen walk around me,
> They walk around me both night and day,
> When they know I got my 44
> They won't have a word to say.
>
> I've made it up in my mind
> And I really don't care how I go.
> Before I'm being mistreated
> I'm going to shoot my 44.

Would Brecht like this? You bet he would. François Villon, too, aspired to be understood by felons.

The most memorable compliment I ever received was in a high school in a New York city slum during a classroom visit. The teacher had xeroxed some of my early poems, like 'Knife', 'My Shoes', 'Fork', and wanted her students to talk about them. Most of them either had no clue or they kept quiet. The two "bad boys who are sure to give you trouble", as the teacher described them, knew exactly what I was up to and told the rest of the class so with an air of contempt. I felt like rolling over like a dog.

How much did you take into later life of that early exposure, through your mother, to opera and classical song?

A lot. There was a time in 1959-61 when I went to the opera at least once a week. I heard all the great voices of the second half of the twentieth century in person. After a few bottles of wine, I've been known to sing Mozart arias. I still listen to the opera, but not as much as I listen to chamber music and solo piano. In fact, I listen to some type of music all the time. My father was like that. He loved Schubert's songs and he adored Argentine tangos. Frankly, I never met anyone with such a wide musical appetite.

Here's a little secret for you. When I was in my teens and my twenties, anytime I had a long walk someplace, I'd spend the time by composing symphonies in my head and humming them as I went along. Every day a new symphony or a concerto – if the walk was long enough. If not, then perhaps only a single movement. I don't have to tell you that I had the highest opinion of my compositions, which I mostly forgot after a week or two. I have several certified lunatics in my family, so that must be the explanation. After I bought my first car, I stopped. I listened to the classics on the radio while driving with one hand and conducting with the other. So my vast musical works, which even include a part of an opera, are completely lost.

You end your memoir 'In the beginning ...' with a moment from a war-time performance of The Marriage of Figaro, *in which Figaro, seeing that Susanna's scarf has accidentally caught fire, swiftly stamps it out "without missing a beat". Is the point of the anecdote that one just has to keep on dealing with things as they happen? (It's possible to read it in other ways, but this reading seems invited since it closes this memoir.)*

Yes, he took it in stride, as if the scariest, the most extraordinary thing had not happened. I could not forget his flair, his presence of mind, the way he kept the comic spirit of the performance uninterrupted while the audience gasped in horror. Outside, the war was on. We were an occupied country. People were arrested, disappeared or were sent to camps. There were public executions. That's how art exists in this world of ours – a clear head in the face of calamity.

Can you see any terms in which you could agree with Pater's view that all art constantly aspires towards the condition of music?

It may aspire to, but it had better not try to carry through the idea. There are the so-called sound poets who break words into syllables and make a "poem" solely out of vowels. It can be interesting, but not as good as listening to birds or a dog howling at the moon. There are many wrong-headed pronouncements about the arts that sound full of promise, but put into practice prove to be a disaster. Like John Cage's idea that there's more music in silence than any music one can compose, or like me saying in the spirit of Mallarmé that the supreme poem is really the blank page. These are pretty notions that sound like the truth but aren't.

A good deal of attention has been focused on the marriage of the European and the American in your poetry. In fact the European strain weakens over the course of time, as one might expect, while American specifics (Bartleby the Scrivener, Kansas or Nebraska, Washington or Lincoln, the little house on the prairie, the common insects of North America) are named with greater frequency, and the texture of everyday life (an old red Chevy on blocks, a cookout, Yankee Pot Roast, a front porch and rocking chair) steadily becomes more palpably American. I'm not so much concerned with the process by which you metamorphosed into an American: it's easy to trace from your writings your youthful enthusiasm for the States, and the beneficial impact your father's attitude had in helping you adapt on arrival, just as it's not difficult to guess that a professorship, a Pulitzer Prize and a MacArthur Fellowship confirm one's sense of acceptance, of being in the right place. But I'd like you to comment as fully as you can on a number of references in your poems which, taken together (and leaving the Second World War aside for the moment), have the effect of associating violence, menace, philosophical and religious intractability or superstition, and the habits and perceptions of folk traditions, with Europe. The references are from the earlier work, up to Austerities.

> *... a dark church*
> *Where they bring the cripple and the imbecile*
> *To be healed.*

Most of my experiences of violence were in Europe, although as everyone knows America is a pretty violent place, so I had plenty of reminders. Why certain images recur and others don't is a mystery. Clearly some things made a bigger impression on me visually than others I couldn't get out of my mind. As to the lines you quote: I remember Puerto-Rican women at work talking about some famous healer in Spanish Harlem, and once or twice seeing such miracle men at work on TV. That whole world of evangelical, fundamentalist Christianity fascinates me. There's also, of course, post-war Belgrade, where so many people were on crutches. And then there were the Vietnam veterans, etc., etc.

an evil-eyed woman spitting into a pail of milk.

A common accusation against witches from Salem, Massachusetts, to Serbia. I read about a commercial agreement the other day for Serbia to sell milk to Croatia, and I thought, aha! I suppose I'm also remembering the old peasant women at open markets in my childhood – toothless crones bent to the ground, but nevertheless sly and sharp-witted.

Old ones to the side.

World War Two scene: the young are off to forced labour, the old into the mass grave. They had a rule in Serbia: for one German killed, one hundred natives get executed. They'd close a street, separate people, count to a hundred, and off they'd go to kill them. The whole war was like that. Someone was always counting heads, letting some people get on the train while leaving others behind, and so forth.

In one [pocket] a crust of bread, in another a sausage.

More wartime Europe, columns of refugees, hunger, misery. To have a sausage was a big thing, more exciting than a meal for two in a four star restaurant in Paris. There's nothing to eat, then all of a sudden someone takes a dry sausage out of their pocket. A miracle!

> *Dürer, I like that horse of yours.*
> *I spent my childhood hidden in his guts.*
> *The knight looks like my father*
> *The day he came out of prison.*

I wanted to make a poem that would be like Dürer's engraving. That's all

I remember about it.

> Grandmothers who wring the necks
> Of chickens; old nuns
> With names like Theresa, Marianne,
> Who pull schoolboys by the ear ...

An evocation of an older world – it could be either Europe or America – which really wasn't mine, but which I liked imagining. Of course, when I was a kid I watched women slaughtering chickens in the courtyard of the apartment house where I lived in Belgrade. There was no choice. You bought them live in the open market, and had to do the rest. Pigs too. I'd be reading a book or playing with my toy soldiers when all of a sudden there'd be the sound of a pig squealing down below, so like everybody else I'd run to the balcony.

> You're the famous torturer much feared
> I beg you to spare my love
> Who is in your darkest prison cell
> I wish to marry him etc.

I have always been amazed by people who torture others – the nice neighbour, always ready to help carry the bag of groceries upstairs for your mother or grandmother, who spends his nights pulling out people's fingernails. The poem reads like a quick plot summary of a longish ballad. It's like I was saying: everybody knows the story, so why tell it at great length?

> I like it when
> Achilles
> Gets killed

Enough epics, tribal heroes, meddling gods and all those clashing spears and swords, the poem says. Let's have some lyric poetry for a change, perhaps about a girl taking a walk in an olive orchard. I'm attacking collective madness and its chest-beating heroes from the point of view of an individual who is fed up with slaughter and the poetry that makes excuses for it.

The Second World War inevitably left its mark on you, and you have given memorable accounts of your boyhood experience of it. Can you comment on the presence of the War behind earlier poems such as 'Prodigy' or 'Travelling Slaughterhouse'?

'Prodigy' is straight autobiography. I did learn to play chess during the war and may have seen people hung from lampposts. 'Travelling Slaughterhouse' is a mix of disconnected memories and images that have little to do with me. I was trying to convey the feel of wartime. I was born in a violent century and grew up in a time of genocide. All I ever heard from my relatives was war, war, war. They'd start a story this way: "After uncle Milivoje lost a leg and the gangrene set in", or "When your grandpa Zica was hiding from Austrian police in 1916", or "When someone else showed up to be inducted wearing a military jacket with pinstripe pants and spats and was threatened with a court martial, and your other uncle came out of a mental hospital wearing a major's uniform with his chest covered with medals", etc. No wonder history interests me. My family has served as its cannon fodder for hundreds of years. In fact, my grandfather's Balkan Wars are preserved forever in Picasso's and Braque's collages of the years 1909-11. If one steps close to the canvasses, one can read the reports of battles in which he fought. However, just as the reports get exciting, Picasso rips off the page and the museum guard comes over to warn you not to stick your nose in a masterpiece.

I have a hunch that it was the writing of the memoir 'In the beginning ...' that finally made it possible for you to approach the subject of the War more directly in your poetry, as you did, say, in the poems 'Two Dogs' and 'The Big War' in The Book of Gods and Devils. *The note of defensive evasiveness that sounded in the 1972 interview you did for* Crazy Horse *(also reprinted in* The Uncertain Certainty*), when you referred in passing to "the usual number of terrifying war experiences", is quite gone now, as is the obliquity with which the War made itself felt in your earlier poetry. Is it right to think it took you some time to be able to deal with the War directly?*

Not really. I shared my top war stories with all my friends long before I started writing them down. With thousands of World War Two memoirs already in existence, I thought: who the hell would be interested in another? Besides, I'm the kid who said the day the war ended, "Now we are not going to have any more fun." When so many others had suffered so much more, it was embarrassing to make a big deal of my encounter with evil. I started writing down these memories after my father and mother passed away, in the realisation that, with our family dying off and being dispersed all over the world, there would be no record left. While they were alive, their memories were all they ever talked about.

Did you ever have the feeling that Americans, who of course played a distinguished part in the Second World War but experienced none of Europe's wholesale destruction on their own soil, were lacking a dimension? (This is a commonly held European view, and may be as misconceived as so many other European ideas about America.)

Sure. It's impossible to imagine someone who had been bombed in the past enthusing about "Bombs for Peace" or "Military Humanism" as we did when we bombed Serbia in 1999. We, Americans, killed literally millions of civilians bombing Germany, Japan, Vietnam, etc., but this has not bothered many people at home since they have no clue what that is like. True, we fought and died in all these wars and many families felt the pain of that loss, but collectively we missed out seeing New York and Washington in smoking ruins.

The poem 'War' in Hotel Insomnia *seems through its last line to equate war with a personified Death, which in turn, by implication, would mean that war is a universal, a factor in every individual life. This implication is so simple as to be finally a little intractable.*

A large percentage of humanity– if not the majority – has been affected by war in the last century. Not many have escaped that common fate. All one has to do is turn on CNN any time, at any hour, to get a confirmation of that. Someone somewhere in the world is lying in a puddle of blood. I realise most people don't notice it or get as upset as I do – and I understand them. My children, too, say I exaggerate, I'm a pain in the ass with my gloom and doom. Well, maybe. Still, killing the innocent seems to me what human beings have always done and still do with great enthusiasm. Look at world history or mythology and what do you find? Murder, rape, imprisonment, or the slitting of some innocent young maiden's throat to appease the god of war.

About the time of The World Doesn't End, *I have a sense of European names – Hermes, Socrates, Nietzsche, Freud, a whole long list down to the dogs named Rimbaud and Hölderlin – being used as ciphers or shorthand, as props in a theatre of words. There is something eerie about the representatives of European culture here, as if they were aspects of a Higher Caricature, the Daumier version of the life of the mind, rather than bearers of an identifiable experiential value. I've wondered why I have this feeling (and whether you would have any idea what I'm talking about). Is it because, by then, the distance in time from the traumatic experiences of the Second World War was sufficient for the pain of Europe to be wearing off? Or is it that the mental distance from Europe was sufficient for the complex cultural history of an entire continent to start simplifying into manageable form?*

These are poets and philosophers I read and continue to read. They are in the poems because they represent for me certain aesthetic and metaphysical ideas, so in that respect they are like actors in a play that is my life. I get up in the morning, shuffle on stage, bump into Socrates on the way to the bathroom and we get into an argument. Today I'm convinced that he and that poet-hater Plato got just about everything wrong. Other times, I grovel before them. What could be more normal when one spends one's life with books? I make jokes at their expense, but I would feel terribly lonely if I didn't have them for company.

Later again, in Hotel Insomnia, *I feel there is a re-engagement with European reality, most appealingly in a very tranquil, beautiful poem, 'The Old World', which places your sense of the experience that precedes words in a Sicilian setting that is very delicate and vivid. Can you say something about the background to and writing of that poem?*

In 1963 I was in Palermo for two days, and that's all I ever saw of Sicily. I remember thinking what an old, old place it was. The poem has more to do with my going off to drink wine alone in the French countryside when I was in the army, and with my other trips to Italy afterwards, than with an actual experience in an actual place. Even some of my most autobiographical sounding poems are really collages of memories or pure inventions.

You're correct, though, about my re-engaging with European reality. These are the consequences of my numerous trips there since 1982. Before that, I knew Paris, Yugoslavia and a few other places superficially. In the last twenty years, I've really roamed around and spent time there.

Food plays a more important part in your poetry than in that of any other poet who comes to mind, except perhaps Günter Grass. Again, it's not hard to grasp that those who underwent the privations of the War and the post-War years would have a sharpened sense of the value and meaning of food (those in my own family who went through the War had the same sense), but in your poetry you assign a heightened significance to kitchens and to the act of cooking, as if to imply a whole sociology of family and friendship as well as sheer relish. Could you expand on this?

What's a poem but a well-prepared dish served on a plate? I love to cook and eat good food, so it is inevitable that there'd be plenty of mentions of it. Besides, isn't eating also one of the fundamental realities of our lives? We all do it two or three times a day, and yet it's rarely present in most literature, except, of course, in Rabelais and Cervantes and other great comic writers. Can one really trust a poet or a metaphysician who never notices the mouth, the belly and the sexual organs, who pretends we live only in the intellect or the imagination? Would Kant have been a better philosopher if he had worried about sausages as much as did about the critique of judgement? Say you're lying sleepless and thinking great thoughts, when all of a sudden you remember that there's one bottle of Guinness left in the refrigerator. That moment of bliss ought to be included alongside whatever lofty ideas you have.

Restaurant settings recur in your poetry. Again a biographical origin is easily traced, but I wonder if you could describe whatever metaphoric or symbolic dimension you find in the restaurant situation.

I don't know about symbolic dimensions. I just love the sight of a solitary customer tucking the napkin in his shirt collar and putting his glasses on to see what is in the soup he has just been served. I have always written in restaurants. It's highly recommended. They are surprised to see you doing so, think maybe you are taking notes on the food, when you are just tinkering with a poem or jotting down various ideas. In the meantime, there's the all-absorbing spectacle of other customers eating and talking while the waiters fuss over them. People-watching is my favourite occupation and there's no better place for that than a restaurant when one is dining alone.

Elias Canetti saw the act of eating meat as the ultimate expression of power, since it means the complete elimination of the other's existence. What part of you, if any, assents to this understanding of eating?

That's just too easy. A farmer loves an animal, kills it and eats with great enjoyment. So, go figure. I don't think cuisine can be reduced to an exercise of power over the lower order of beings.

Describing your reading of Neruda, you wrote: "It's a poetry that makes me happy. I want to go out and live life to the fullest, eat an enormous meal, drink wine with friends, stay up all night long, and then for breakfast make a big tomato salad with onions, basil, and green peppers from the garden." It's a more wonderful response to poetry than whole libraries of criticism. Is this Simic paradise?

It's as close as I have ever got to one. Obviously, not all poetry has that effect. I can't imagine having that same reaction to Dickinson or Frost, who are much greater poets, but with Neruda or Whitman it's our senses that get roused up. You want to stuff yourself, drink, walk all night in the city, screw, sit on a Manhattan rooftop watching the sun come up and ask yourself what does it all mean and believe for a moment that you have an answer.

Those green peppers – would you yourself have been the gardener who grew them?

Sad to say, my peppers are usually inferior. I have too many rocks and trees in my yard, but I have kind neighbours who have more sunlight, better soil and are far better gardeners, who bring them to me, for which I kiss them and serve them my best wines.

In describing his requirements of students in an ideal poetry academy, Auden suggested that each should be required to tend a garden plot or care for a domestic animal. What would be your own other requirements for those students?

In addition, I'd teach them how to cook. Of course, they'd have to spend the first few years chopping garlic, onions, parsley, and washing dishes. Then I'd introduce them gradually to the mysteries of the frying pan into which a few drops of olive oil have been introduced. When they learn that grilling squid is as tricky as composing a sonnet, I'll issue them a license to practice poetry, with my greasy thumbprint as the official seal.

I'd like to ask about one or two individual poems that I feel have a special importance in your evolution as a poet. Going back to Dismantling the Silence, *there's the extraordinary 'Butcher Shop', which seems to re-capitulate so much of your early experience (blood, superstition, the store windows you'd stop at on your long walks while playing truant from school), but at the same time has a resonance entirely distinct from the personal. Do you recall how you arrived at this poem, and particularly the shifting perspective of the final quatrain, and the voice?*

This is one of the earliest poems of mine that I kept. I don't remember how I wrote it. What I recall are old Ukrainian and Polish butcher shops on the Lower East Side of Manhattan. I walked past them many times, at all hours of the day, since I had friends in that neighbourhood. This was 1958-59. Many of my poems come out of such experiences. I saw something and it nagged me, sometimes for many years. I'm surprised I pulled it off, since I had little skill in those days. I probably wrote it late at night in one of the flea-bag hotels I used to stay in.

The object poems in the same collection, about a fork, a knife, a spoon, a stone, and so forth – you mentioned them a little earlier – have attracted a lot of comment. In your 'Notes on Poetry and Philosophy', you yourself make the link to Husserl, and to the Imagists. Is there not also an affinity with the Rilke of the New Poems, *around 1902-08, when he was writing of objects animate and inanimate in the hope of rendering the* ding an sich?

That came after. My original reason was simply to be irreverent. You want something poetic? A poem about the glories of nature or the confessions of a sensitive suffering soul? I'll give you a poem about a fork or a pair of old shoes. I had read the American and European modernist poets, so I knew it had been already done in a certain way, but not in the way I intended to do it. The knowledge that there were no poems in existence about forks, knives, spoons and the other things I wrote about, excited me tremendously. I was strictly on my own. Inevitably, I received a letter from the editor of a literary magazine to which I had sent the object poems, asking me why I wasted my time writing about things so lacking in poetry.

Aside from that, I think any time one sets out to describe an object, one is asking questions about the nature of seeing. Description is not only a surreptitious portrait of the author but is also a form of epistemological inquiry.

And yes, in the process one hopes to capture some essential quality of the object.

One German critic well described those poems of Rilke's as an attempt to experience things so intensely that the absolute became apparent in them, and I'm reminded of your comment that the object poems are about the absolute. Or rather, "the absolute otherness of the object". Which in turn seems at variance with your observation on awe (as in

Dickinson) being *"the beginning of metaphysics: that is, awe at the multiplicity of things and awe at their suspected unity". Does the point of such writing finally lie in the attempt to reconcile "absolute otherness" with "suspected unity"?*

That's very, very good, Michael. That's the cross I'm crucified upon. On the one hand, the suspicion of that otherness in its terrifying remoteness and distance from any meaning, and, on the other hand, the suspicion that all things are connected and we are part of something we cannot name. They can't be both true – or could they be? Which one do I believe in? It depends on what day of the week you happen to ask me. Dickinson could not make up her mind if the universe had a God, or whether it was just infinite and mostly empty space. That's where I feel closest to her. It seems to me that it is important to experience this contradiction fully, rather than to try to resolve it. That paradox is the only absolute I'm sure of.

To what extent were the object poems a defiant response to the kind of logical positivism you wrote of in 'Reading Philosophy at Night' ("the poet in me rebels and I want to write a poem about an intelligent pencil in love with music")?

Poetry is often criticism of the way certain poets and philosophers think about the world. One reads something that strikes one as either all wrong or only partly true. I think Wallace Stevens wrote many of his poems to argue with Emerson, William James, W.C. Williams and others. Logical positivists and Marxists and many poets have kept me up at night fuming. That's where I part company with Europe. I have no conversations with the Serbian and French poetic traditions, but I certainly have with the American one. I take personally what I regard as insults to its spirit.

The poem 'errata' reads like a joke, or maybe a phenomenological joke if we take it too seriously, but it has an interesting ending: "my greatest mistake / the word I allowed to be written / when I should have shouted / her name". You've never been fooled, have you, about which is the greater, Life or Art? Life, plainly.

That poem comes at the end of a badly flawed group of poems that I never reprinted. I wanted to provide errata for the universe I had just created. Then in the very last line of my errata, it occurred to me that instead of playing games here, I should have shouted the name of my love. My conviction is that poetry needs life and the presence of real human beings to keep renewing itself. Poetry left to itself has no content to explore. It says over and over again, How strange to be writing this poem. This is not only an impoverishment of what poetry is capable of, it is also very boring. I love literature and art as much as anyone else, but I also love life in all its messiness. Every time I'm in New York, I ask myself: How come there are poets living here who never mention the city? In fact, this is true of most of them. And yet, if one opens one's eyes and ears, this is one of the most astonishing places in the world.

Of 'Brooms' in Return to a Place Lit by a Glass of Milk *you later said that it was writing this poem that taught you that an object is "an encyclopaedia of archetypes". Isn't it rather that an object serves to set in motion the mind's habit of making associations, and taking pleasure in itself doing so?*

That's what I meant. The encyclopaedia is in our heads. I didn't realise how thick it was, how many pages it had, till I looked at an ordinary kitchen broom.

The poem on your own name has an affinity with Tomaz Salamun's rather darker 'History', which begins "Tomaz Salamun is a monster" and ends, in a manner very like what American and British readers now think of as the Simic manner: "This is Tomaz Salamun, he went to the store / with his wife Marushka to buy some milk. / He will drink it and this is history." In the introduction to the Salamun selection which you edited and half-translated, Robert Hass made a remark on this poem which struck me as very apt not just to Salamun but also to yourself: "The solution he had found ... to any problem of cultural loneliness was the one Walt Whitman had found to his personal loneliness in Brooklyn." Does this strike a chord with you?

I don't think I knew Tomaz's poem when I wrote mine, but I could be wrong. Most likely we have both gotten the idea from the Serbian poet Matija Belckovic, who had a book called *Thus Spake Matija* in 1965 that mocked the manner of Nietzsche's *Zarathustra*.

As for the second part of your question, I'm usually not the hero of my poems in the way Tomaz is of his. This may sound odd, but I have no interest in telling the story of my life or creating a consistent persona in my poems. I'm far more interested in lying, that is, playing with a variety of fictional viewpoints with their accompanying psychologies and beliefs.

The problem is that, any time one uses the first-person pronoun, the reader assumes it's the author spilling the goods. Otherwise, I like what Hass says about Whitman and Salamun and only wish that were the case with me, but it is not, unless I have inadvertently done the opposite of what I intended. That happens, of course.

You referred somewhere to the long poem 'White' as being a sequence of ghazals, which I take it means ghazals in the North American under-standing of recent decades rather than in the original Persian sense. Could you say something about how and why it mattered to cast the poem in this form, and which practitioners of the form shaped your own use of it?

They may have started as ghazals, with whatever notion I had of the form from reading Bly, Rich and Jim Harrison, but after thirty years of revising 'White', I have no clear sense of what it has become. There are twenty poems, each one consisting of five couplets. That's not much room for anything to happen, so I thought I would create tension by having huge semantic gaps between couplets for the reader to bridge with his imagination. Or, one could say, I wanted to make short lyric poems by collaging fragments. 'White' exists in at least five different published versions. In the final one it is much less fragmentary, I believe, and despite some remaining awkward spots it hopefully works better.

At the close of the poem 'Charon's Cosmology', in the collection of the same title, I feel that the "dark river / Swift and cold and deep" is close to the water at the close of Elizabeth Bishop's great poem, 'At the Fishhouses': "dark, salt, clear, moving, utterly free, / drawn from the cold hard mouth / of the world". How do you read Bishop's poem? Do you agree with Seamus Heaney's account of it, in The Redress of Poetry*?*

I know Bishop's poem well, but not Heaney's essay. In any case, it's not a conscious allusion on my part to the ending of her poem. My Charon is in a pickle. After centuries of ferrying the dead, he's forgotten and is now unable to tell which bank of the river Styx is which since there are identical piles of corpses on both sides. He keeps going through the motions, but he suspects that he may have reversed the direction. There are just too many dead in the world for one mythical ferryman to manage alone. As for the river, I wanted to make it as real as possible, the kind of river you'd find in northern New England, where I live; so perhaps the nearly identical landscape gives the impression that I was alluding to her poem.

The philosophical joking comes thicker and faster round about the time of Classic Ballroom Dances *and* Austerities, *in poems like 'Bedtime Story', 'The Childhood of Parmenides' or 'Madonnas Touched up with a Goatee'. Your reputation as a philosophical poet has done you no harm, even with a reading public that would normally run a mile when the name of Heidegger is mentioned, no doubt because you have an engagingly concrete and enthusiastic way of writing about the pleasures of philosophy. Also, the fact is that Heidegger and Husserl may have tempered your mind, but you don't engage their philosophy or their language directly in your poetry. Which is a mercy. In what sense, given what you've written about the nature of thinking in poetry, do you recognise the possibility of "philosophical" poetry?*

I certainly recognize the possibility – Stevens and Rilke got away with it – but I prefer the way Frost, Dickinson and Stevens (in his short poems) do their thinking. Let me put it this way: philosophical questions as subject matter of poems and the abstract rhetoric that goes with it are less interesting to me than metaphors and images where idea, emotion and the senses are all together. If a poet starts with a philosophical idea – no matter how brilliant – and uses the poem to illustrate it, I say forget it. That's the way ministers write their Sunday sermons. Philosophy asks "What is Being?" Poetry attempts to create the experience of being for the reader. "No ideas, but in things," as Williams said. Poets are always worrying about particulars. There's also our reliance on the imagination over reason. If poets end up being metaphysicians, it's almost despite themselves. I mean, first beauty, then truth. A poem, when it works, is first of all an aesthetic experience, an experience in which one is in no rush to separate and abstract the meaning. Another way of putting this is to say that what truly interests me is the radically different ways in which poets and philosophers think.

It struck me as I was looking through your poetry for the philosophers, the recognisable concepts, and so forth, that in fact the saints, mystics and divines easily outnumber the Hegels, Schopenhauers, Nietzsches and assorted Greeks. Leaving aside figures from the New Testament in particular (Jesus Christ, Mary, Mary Magdalene, Joseph, Judas and others), I find Bernard of Clairvaux, Thomas Aquinas, and a variety of other saints (Isaac, Nilus, Francis, John of the Cross, Theresa of Avila), Julian of Norwich, Albertus Magnus, Meister Eckhart, Jakob Boehme, and, above all, Pascal. As if anyone could have doubted it, this confirms that the struggle with God has been one of the great centres of your intellectual and spiritual life. Do you dare to agree with the words of Pascal that you quote in 'Mystic Life': "In that thou hast sought me, / Thou hast already found me"?

One has to respect both philosophers and religious mystics, since they both seek the absolute. Some of them are convinced that they have found it, but I have not. In the meantime, I'm happy to read what they have to say, and I'm often deeply moved and nearly persuaded by them. If I refer to them by name in my poems, it is because they are a part of my argument with myself. The old quarrel between philosophy and poetry is bad enough, but when it comes to poetry and theology, it's our very soul that is at stake. I never believed in heaven, but hell is a distinct possibility. So I flail, run around in circles, and frequently contradict myself. I'm always saying to myself, well, this fellow sounds kind of convincing, but on the other hand …

It is difficult to work out whether you find yourself able to believe in God. In the 1972 interview I referred to earlier, you say unambiguously, "I don't mind admitting that I believe in God." Less clearly in your own authentic voice is a brief note in the title piece of Wonderful Words, Silent Truth: *"What a mess! I believe in images as vehicles of transcendence, but I don't believe in God!" Still less clear, since the words are in a poem not necessarily the product of an egotistical sublime, is the address to "You in whom I do not believe" in the second of your poems titled 'Psalm' (the one in* A Wedding in Hell*); but just a few pages on in the same book, in the poem 'Prayer', you not only capitalise "You" once again but write, for all your reservations, the words "O Lord". It seems to me that you have the temperament of a believer, and the honesty of a believer plagued by never-ending doubts. Do you feel able to say what your present thinking is on this matter of God, and how you would describe the milestones along your road to that position?*

I haven't budged from the description you just gave. I believe in the irresoluble mystery, the supreme enigma, and the unnameable cause of everything existing. I have in mind an X, not the God of my great-grandfather, who like many of my ancestors was a priest. This "God" of mine is remote, permanently "out to lunch". I learned to blaspheme at the dinner table of my grandparents and parents, who were fed up with priests, starting with the ones in our family. Remember, Eastern Orthodox priests marry and have to put up with nagging wives and doubting offspring. And, I understand what being devout means. I'll happily bow my head in any church, but I find official church doctrines laughable. Two years ago, one worried reader in North Carolina sent me his own Bible without a comment. He could see I was a sinner in need of salvation because I keep saying in one breath that God does and does not exist.

There's an extremely important and beautiful poem on this question, it seems to me, in Jackstraws, a poem which I'd nominate as one of the very few fully serious and fully wondrous religious poems of our times. You describe in 'De Occulta Philosophia' the experience of evening sunlight, the sense of being granted "A small share in some large / And obscure knowledge", and of wanting to know more. The "you" to whom "Your humble servant" addresses this poem is characterised as preferring solitude, gravity, severity and reserve, and is addressed, "Oh supreme unknowable". From this "you" it is possible to learn "so much" and "absolutely nothing". Questions about the position this poem takes will almost certainly have been answered in your replies to the last two questions, but here I'd like additionally to know, first, why the poem takes its title from a cuss-headed work of mysticism and magic by Agrippa von Nettesheim; second, whether it is right to associate it with Emily Dickinson's 'There's a certain Slant of light' and the sense in that poem, on which you have written movingly, of witnessing a sacred mystery; and third, whether we haven't in fact come full circle here, to that profound sense of silence you've spoken of since the early years of your writing life, that maternal silence of which poetry is "an orphan"?

I'm glad this poem works for you. There's something indeed occult and magical about evening sunlight, so I remembered that wonderful title of that foolish book. You are also right to bring in Dickinson. This is an attempt to describe the feeling that the visible world is about to reveal its secret to us. I'm asking the light and the silence: "How come you give the impression you know so much? And if you do, indeed, know something, I pray that you teach it to me." In late summer, here where I live, the birds no longer sing at sunset and a deep peace reigns in the countryside. In the poem it's getting dark. I'm watching the light wane, too spellbound to get up and turn on the light. So, just as one is about to be enlightened, as it were, the night falls. I'm sitting in the dark thinking: Well, what was it that I just understood?

Your great attachment to the things of this world must be, at one and the same time, a help and a hindrance in seeking belief. I was struck by something you wrote about Benjamin Péret some twenty years ago: "If

Péret has a 'metaphysics', it has to do with the interdependence of love and the marvellous. Each of his images is as earthbound as the act of love." To what extent do you recognise yourself in that description?

I suppose I do. Sex, eroticism and love is where it all begins for me. They make my imagination run wild and nothing can be created or understood without imagination. I think I became a poet at the age of nine or ten when I lay in my bed for hours one night unable to sleep while trying to imagine what was under the dress of a beautiful, much older girl who had just moved across the street from us in Belgrade. I met her almost every day and spent my nights imagining our life together. What I imagined was so marvellous, I was sorry it did not exist outside of my head. It took me a few more years to realise there was a way to have her outside my head too. I could write a poem about her.

In what way, in your understanding, does belief in God differ from agreement with Husserl (whom you cite on this in your 1984 piece, 'A Clear and Open Place') that "the living present is the ultimate, universal and absolute form of transcendental experience"?

To experience the present moment fully is a kind of epiphany. It's the one truth all Eastern and Western mystics agree on. Only in the present do we partake of divinity. Most of us, unfortunately, are half-asleep most of the time, dreaming about the past or dreaming about the future. We are everywhere except where we ought to be, and that is here and now. That consciousness is godlike is an old idea. It has always made perfect sense to me.

There is one last question in this complex that you have raised or cited explicitly on more than one occasion in your work: why is there something rather than nothing? To which another question must be joined: in what spirit can readers seek from a poet replies (as if they were possible) to the questions that defeat theology and physics?

Because poets are nuts! In their heart of hearts, they believe they can do just that, give you the real truth, the kind you can't get anywhere else. No wonder philosophers are always warning against them. "Unacknowledged legislators of the world" – can you believe that crap? Take a look at American poets: Whitman, Dickinson, Frost, Stevens and even Williams. They went off and each constructed their own model of the universe. No other one was good enough for them. If there's a hell, it's so crowded with poets, they have to relocate other sinners to heaven since there's no room down below.

I'd like you to comment on some of the words that recur with relative frequency in your poetry ...

Sure, but bear in mind that while some words and images have greater significance for me than others do – it's like that with every poet I ever read closely – this isn't to say that I think of them as having fixed meanings, where they represent a particular idea or symbol. Rather, they are open-ended in terms of their connotations. They reappear because they feed my imagination.

First, "snow" ...

We have long snowy winters. It snows here from November to April, so there's no choice. If we had palm trees, I'd write about them. As Marianne Moore would say, I have real toads in my imaginary gardens.

"vanishing point" ...

I like geometry and its clarities. I find Euclid very poetic. It's amazing when one comes upon a long street that stretches to a vanishing point. For a city boy that's a vision of heaven.

"naked" ...

I'm just reminding the reader of the fundamental reality of our lives, be it in bed, in the shower, under the doctor's knife on the operating table, in the morgue, etc.

"masks" ...

They intrigue me, always have. Everything from the ones made for Halloween to the more elaborate ones used in theatre and ritual in various cultures. Psychologically we all wear masks also, but immigrants wear so many they have no memory what their original face looked like.

"crutches" ...

Wartime imagery. Go to Bosnia or Serbia today and you'll see people on crutches everywhere.

"waiter" ...

I have had many unforgettable conversations with waiters in my lifetime. We spoke in brief phrases punctuated by long silences – like a Zen Master and his slow-witted pupil – but they taught me a great many things about food and wine.

"wine" ...

I drink it every day, like my father did, so it's hard not to mention it in poems. By the way, is there anything more beautiful than a naked woman with a glass of red wine in her hand?

"dog" ...

I've owned many dogs and own one now. The village I live in is full of dogs. We all know each other and meet daily as I go on my walks in the company of my dog.

"fortune-teller" ...

Like masks, I adore them. Madam Olga reading the palm of a shy young man in a storefront late at night. She's telling him the future, all his loves and miseries to come. What could be more poignant than that?

In addition to being the motif that unifies the collection Hotel Insomnia, *insomnia has been referred to throughout your poetry, from the Seventies to* Jackstraws, *and you've written of the existential and mystical condition that is present around Sappho's insomnia. Am I right in thinking you to be a chronic sufferer? If so, what dimensions has the experience contributed to your thinking, and to your poetry?*

A whole lot. I spend eternities lying in the dark and mulling things over. I don't turn on the lights or read or watch TV as others do. I find if I stay quietly in bed, I can still function the next day. One moment I'm worrying how to pay bills, the next moment it's the idiocies of our national politics, and so on. All that tossing and turning has made me the person I am, so it had to influence my poetry. Your beloved is snoring away next to you while you go over your life. Sooner or later you are bound to realise you are all alone in the world and have always been, despite appearances. It's both terrifying and exhilarating. It's a perfect incentive to get up at some wee hour and write a poem, but I don't. I stay put.

Can you explain what you understand by authenticity in poetry?

A bunch of lies that sound like the truth. Authenticity is the end result and not something one starts with. It's not an easy quality to define, especially if you are convinced, as I am, that in poetry one ought to be open to any surprise. In any case, it has nothing to do with sincerity and personal integrity, as we know. A full commitment to the art of poetry helps, by which I mean the fear of faking it, of not being oneself, of doing sloppy work, of not honouring your poetic ancestors.

I'd like to ask about some more individual poems that strike me as having a special importance in your work. In Unending Blues *you have an extravagantly theatrical performance, 'For the Sake of Amelia', which is rather more luridly over-the-top than the manner you mostly choose. What were you aiming to do in this poem?*

I wish I knew. The poem just took off, then got crazier and crazier, and I went along for the ride. I have no memory of writing it. My guess is I wanted something extravagant and cinematic in the manner of Fellini and Pasolini at their most magical.

'The Fly' reads like an amiable nod to Miroslav Holub's poem of the same title, though it's a rather more complex poem. Were you deliberately "answering" Holub?

I wasn't, although I love Holub's poem. I have a lot of flies in my poems because the little pests have always interested me, not to mention that when one is alone with no one to talk to in the city, a fly is most welcome. When *Jackstraws* came out, there were so many bugs in it, my friends were beginning to ask behind my back, "What's going on here? Has Charlie been guzzling too much wine lately?" The answer lies elsewhere. In my old age – if that's what being over sixty is? – I've become fascinated with insects. When I was a kid, like any normal child, I'd run and step on an ant the moment I saw one. Now I'll watch it forever. I like flowers, and my wife grows many varieties of them in our yard, but I never look at them closely. Give me an absent-minded ant who keeps stopping again and again and retracing his steps, and I'm in heaven.

Another poem in Unending Blues, *'Birthday Star Atlas', is a product of your relationship with Emily Dickinson, one of poetry's more unlikely love affairs (at first glance)? Can you say something about what Dickinson has given you?*

Well, where shall I begin? She writes short poems and I write short poems. She speculates about ultimate things and so do I. She thrives on paradoxes and contradictions and so do I. She's very smart and says things that to me sound absolutely true. For instance, "Death sets a Thing significant / The Eye had Hurried by." Finally, she is capable of breathtaking visionary moments, like when she writes:

> I saw no Way – The Heavens were stitched –
> I felt the Columns close –
> The Earth reversed her Hemispheres –
> I touched the Universe –
>
> And back it slid – and I alone –
> A speck upon a Ball –
> Went out opon Circumference –
> Beyond the Dip of Bell –

I like her independence and her intellectual integrity. She doesn't make it easy on herself. She thinks things through and follows their consequences. She intuits a connection between psychology and cosmology and worries about it. She is capable of both blasphemy and deepest reverence. What I'm saying is: she is very complicated and close to my heart.

I know some Europeans don't believe me when I say that I feel at home in the New England tradition with its Calvinism and Emerson's Transcendentalism. My favourite writers, the ones I have taught and reread for more than thirty years, are, in addition to Dickinson and Emerson, Thoreau, Hawthorne, Melville, William James and Frost. Dickinson herself felt like an outsider and so do I for obvious reasons. Still, their world is much closer to me now than that of Vasko Popa. He told me that himself the last time I saw him. He knew I was not a Serbian poet. It shocked me when he said it. Not that I had any ambitions in that direction; still, I didn't realize what I had become till that moment.

'The Little Pins of Memory', the poem that opens The Book of Gods and Devils, *seems as close as you get to solving the problem of putting the*

synchronicity of experience into sequential language. Is the poetic image, with all its vagaries, the moment in which time is cancelled out and past and present become co-existent?

Yes, definitely. Every great image aspires to be a holy icon of its mother tongue – a wonder-working icon, I had better add. No one has ever figured out how images, metaphors and other figures of speech come into being. We know imagination has a way of detecting previously unperceived resemblances, but how? And why in some circumstances and not in others? It's a puzzle that no one has solved, because it has nothing to do with operations of our rational mind or even our psychology. So, I don't know how that synchronicity comes about. It is my ideal, but my wanting it doesn't mean I'm going to get it. There's no recipe for how to concoct a memorable image. Poetry is a kind of alchemy in which the alchemist works in the dark with unknown materials.

One of the funniest moments in contemporary poetry, at least for my sense of humour, is at the end of 'St Thomas Aquinas' in the same book: "'I'm Bartleby the Scrivener,' I told the Italian waiter. / 'Me, too,' he replied." Taking a good joke too seriously, can we have the Simic pocket view of the nature of individual identity?

Without a doubt. The waiter in question is the type who agrees with everything the customer says. He has no idea who Bartleby is, or that he is one too, or that Manhattan is full of Bartlebies. Of course, this is an immigrant scene. Go ahead and call me what you want and I'll be that too. Like at Ellis Island. You were originally called Mr Poklekowski and you became Mr Parker with a stroke of a pen.

The Book of Gods and Devils *contains your only attempt in poetry to broach that pronoun you've seen as so important and enigmatic, "it". This "it" is the inexpressible, even the awesome, but it can't help feeling like a bit of a tease as well, since a mere function of language has been elevated into a quasi-mystical role. Can you expand on our habit of attributing special, heightened significance to selected words or sounds?*

That's inevitable. There are words that say more to us than others, words that have magical powers. As for the pronoun "it", here's how I see its origins. In the beginning there was only *it*, since we didn't dare give *it* a name. Eventually, different kinds of *it* were given the names of gods and goddesses, so when we use the pronoun we relive the time when we did not dare name various divinities.

Would the pronoun "it" still possess the same meaning for you when translated into another language?

It's even spookier in Serbo-Croatian and Russian. I once jokingly wrote a paper in a linguistics course claiming that these sentences where *it* is the subject are remnants of earlier times when it was prudent not to name the agent of some natural phenomenon. My theory assumed that in older Russian there would be more of these constructions. My teacher was greatly impressed, wanted to have my paper published. A few years later I ran into him on Park Avenue one night and he told me with great excitement that I was dead wrong, that these constructions have proliferated in the Soviet Union. He expected me to be crushed, but I came up with an instant explanation. "Professor," I told him, "in the days of Stalin, the prudence exercised had to be even greater." I left him thinking that one over.

In The Unemployed Fortune-Teller *you suggest that your feeling "that language is inadequate when speaking about experience is really a religious idea, what they call negative theology". Can you comment more closely on the religious dimension of the relation between language and the given, and on George Steiner's position, in* Real Presences, *that the meaning of meaning is a transcendent postulate?*

This is a reaction to the widely held view today that everything is language. It almost is, but not everything. One cannot really describe the experience of consciousness at its most intense, nor can one do much better with the way my cat is looking at me right now. Do sudden amazement and awe have words? No, they are a form of eloquence that doesn't need them. This is not just a wild notion for me: I feel it, always have. My hunch is that this is what lies at the heart of the religious impulse: an abyss and a silence.

You're a devotee of Heidegger. It's often rather troubled me that much of Heidegger's philosophy is thinking-by-wordplay, and evaporates once it quits the German language: the all-important distinction between Sein *and* Dasein, *for instance, is a distinction that presents itself foremost to a person who inhabits a German universe. What are your own views, not least as a distinguished translator yourself, on the problem of receiving other writers' philosophy or poetry via a language they didn't conceive them in and to which, in some sense, they may finally be exterior or extrinsic?*

It's a problem. I don't know German, so I have read their philosophers and poets in translations. I assume that quite a bit is lost. On the other hand, I don't lose any sleep over it, since what can I or anyone else do about it except learn the language? I'm sure Homer is better in Greek and *The Upanishads* are glorious in the original, but life is short, etc. Neither do I accept that notion, beloved by nationalists everywhere, that with every language comes a unique world-view. Yes, Eskimos have all those nuances in their language about snow and we don't. Still, despite its seeming impossibility, translation does take place and Chinese poets and Spanish poets do understand each other.

Remaining with Heidegger for a moment: do you experience a difficulty in separating the abstract thinking of philosophers you admire from the possibly more questionable areas of their political inclinations? In cases where a similar difficulty arises with poets, such as that of Pound, is it fair to say that the present intellectual climate largely solves the problem by looking the other way?

I never had any doubt that Heidegger was a piece of shit, and so was Pound, whose great poems I still teach. I've never been a blindly worshipping type. There are first-rate philosophical ideas in Heidegger and many questionable ones. That's all that interests me.

Maybe I imagine it, but it seems to me that in the Nineties, around the time of Hotel Insomnia, *a more introspective, meditative note entered your poetry, the note of a man perhaps more alert than before not only to the questions of transcendence – which we've already glanced at – but also, I feel, to his own mortality. Was there a reason for this slight shift? Or do you perhaps not see it that way yourself?*

After fifty, to one's great surprise, one starts going to funerals and visiting friends in hospitals on regular basis. I'm a cheerful sort, but little by little I started to get the idea that I won't live forever. It's different thinking about death at the age of twenty, when you can still stay up all night drinking and raising hell, and when you are sixty-three and have just received a telephone call about another friend passing away or woken up with aches and pains. It would be a little odd if one did not become introspective.

There's a very striking (unrhymed, unmetred) 'Romantic Sonnet' in Hotel Insomnia which leaves me rather regretting your comment elsewhere that one way you overcome the blank page is to write a sonnet, say – the implication being that this mechanical act will do to warm up, before the serious writing gets going. Isn't it a pity to be so off-hand with a form that was good enough for Michelangelo, Shakespeare and Rilke? Is there no chance that Simic might show what he can do in the sonnet form, maybe in his mellow older age ... ?

I was just trying to be funny and it came out stupid. I worship the sonnet form and its masters, and have done variations on it all my life, and may yet do some in traditional meter and rhyme.

In the prose volumes that have accompanied the poetry publications since the mid-Eighties, it emerges that you keep notebooks and that (judging by the selections you publish) these notes have a pronounced tendency toward a quixotically epigrammatic manner that I think of as central European (Kafka and Canetti come to mind). Many of the notes are self-evidently prose, but at times they might be read as singularly short poems (e.g. "O beau pays! The monkey at the typewriter."). When a donnée such as this presents itself, how do you determine whether it will remain a note or evolve into something more?

It usually remains just a brief note. Something pops into my head and it either spurs me to elaborate or it doesn't, but that's where my poems come from. I'm always taking notes since my brain is like a room full of hornets, and this is a way of opening the windows. I first included them in a book as a filler. I didn't have enough pages of prose. Then people told me they are fun to read. I'm always surprised later that some of them actually make sense. Basically, I like fragments, nailing some issue quickly in a sentence or two. Unless there is that informal quality, the spark is missing and it sounds like one is just showing off.

One note of the Nineties begins, "The Gestapo and the KGB were also convinced that the personal is political," where that "also" suggests that you have the totalitarian exactions of extreme political correctness in mind. From various observations, especially about the relation of criticism to the imagination, it's clear you're somewhat out of sympathy with the intellectual climate of the past two or three decades. Could you describe your main grounds for disaffection?

There's no choice. Many of the ideas happily disseminated by American academics have a history of which they do not seem aware. That's where my East European background comes in. Like, wait a minute, I've heard that crap before. If the personal is, indeed, political, then these folks are closer to the persecutors of Akhmatova and Mandelstam than they are to the work of these poets. Understand me. A KGB big shot would find the idea congenial and its rejection worthy of a long stay in Gulag.

Aside from that, I don't care for "lunatics of one idea", as Stevens called them, people who think Lacan or Derrida or somebody else has all the answers and deserves to be worshipped. It's no wonder that, when some Hitler or Stalin comes along, intellectuals and professors are the first in line to kiss their arse. I teach my students to be out of sympathy with their times, in other words not to be sheep.

Are you suggesting an intellectual lineage running from Stalinism and other forms of totalitarian thinking into a Derrida or Lacan? I'd share plenty of reservations about these gentlemen, but rejecting them in these terms seems unnecessarily harsh. Do you want to substantiate this?

No, of course not. You won't believe this, but I used to teach critical theory for years. Derrida and Lacan don't bother me at all. I object to blind followers, dogmatists and enthusiasts of some trendy ideology and enemies of independence and imagination and hence of literature. That type has always been around. Most American academics are insecure about their identity, so they behave like groupies of whatever is intellectually fashionable, while the poets and novelists are not. They may not be very smart, but they usually know who they are. There's the source of the quarrel.

While we're on the subject of the Eastern European experience of political extremity, this is probably as good a moment as any to ask you about your feelings as Yugoslavia disintegrated and the peoples that had lived together for decades took to mass slaughter. I'm especially interested – with a piece you wrote for the London Review of Books *at the back of my mind – in your reactions to the positions Serbs both found themselves in and placed themselves in, throughout the Nineties. To what extent were you able, or willing, or anxious, to identify with Serbian conduct during that period? To what extent did you feel Serbs were misrepresented in North American and western European reporting? What were your views of the merits of the different ethnic claims? How much of you was still able to feel, or wanted to feel, "Serbian", despite your long-standing iden-*

First, let me answer about feeling Serbian. My late father and mother thought of themselves as Yugoslavs. If anyone asked what they were, they would say that they were Yugoslavs. Like millions of suckers from former Yugoslavia, they believed that their ethnic identity came second. And so did I. As you know, I translated poets from all the former republics. I felt myself a part of that country which I was later told was an artificial creation, nothing but a prison house for various nationalities, run by Serbs and for Serbs only. In the 1990s, both in Yugoslavia and in the West, the question of ethnic identity became supreme. All of a sudden, everyone wanted to know what I really was. It was like telling someone you are an American, and he replies, no, you are an Irishman or a Jew and that's *all* you really are. Every tribe in Yugoslavia had its nationalism and the first thing they all did was to examine your ethnic credentials. "Why is Simic, who is supposed to be a Serb, translating Croatian poets? He must have Croatian blood, or, even worse, the enemies of Serbia – the Vatican and the CIA – are paying him huge sums to do that." You've no idea the imbecilities I've read or heard said about me, because I didn't want to get down on my knees and thank God for being a Serb and only a Serb and make excuses for their murders. That's what a true patriot is supposed to do everywhere – claim that all our crimes are justified.

Then, on the other hand, I'd open the papers here in the United States and again get pissed off. Journalists hate complex situations. They like pieces a lynch mob can understand. So I'd read outright lies, stating, for instance, that Marshal Tito, who ruled Yugoslavia for forty years, was a Serb. I guess to admit that he was a Croat would make the reader a bit puzzled about this total Serbian domination. And so it went. One moment I'd be reading an article in the Belgrade press about the collective evil of Croats, Albanians or Bosnians, and then I'd read articles in the United States declaring that Serbs are collectively guilty for crimes committed in their name. I'm talking about leading articles in *The New York Times* and *The New Republic*, which basically said that fascist ideas are acceptable in the case of Serbs. It shocked me. I thought we were sensitive to racism and would never go that route again. So, as you can imagine, I jumped out of my skin.

I suffered more as an American than as a Serb. I hate to see such moral and intellectual shabbiness. Often I could not see any difference between our opportunists and those in the former Yugoslavia, and said so in public. All I had to do, I pointed out, was change the names of the ethnic group in their pieces and they could be published in either place. Saying that was anathema, since our journalists regarded themselves as models of virtue and integrity.

As for the merits of the claims of various ethnic groups, there were plenty of genuine ones on all sides, but that's exactly where the problem lies. Every nationality had a sob story and denied the evil they had done to others. Once you start thinking of ethnic rights solely, rather than individual rights, there's no end to recrimination. I'm dopey enough still to believe in equal rights and justice for all citizens regardless of their ethnic or religious affiliation. Yugoslavia with its millions of faults was nevertheless a multi-ethnic society where that possibility existed in the future. The approach of the West to the crisis emphasised tribal rather than individual rights. In other words, they repudiated their own democratic values. They said, "This here is a good tribe and this here is a bad tribe", as if they were in nineteenth-century Africa. When the bad tribe kills, it's going to be genocide; when the good tribe does the same, we'll pretend it didn't happen, or we'll have our journalist make excuses for them.

What else can I tell you? Serbian conduct was moronic from day one. The moment I saw and heard Milosevic, I knew a blood-bath was on the way. Friends are puzzled that I did so, and so early on. It took no mental effort whatsoever. I was thinking of the United States. Let's say our Anglo-Saxons decide they don't want to live with the rest of us any more. We are all intermixed, of course, but some politician comes along and says: "That's no problem, we'll just do a little ethnic cleansing and live happily ever after." What would you say to people who thought that was a great idea? Or imagine listening to someone explain that English literature is nothing but an apology for genocide? So, yes, it was easy to go absolutely nuts.

To return briefly to one of these questions: how strong did the sense of yourself as (originally) Serbian become during the Yugoslavian break-up and in the aftermath?

Very much. All of a sudden, there were the so-called experts on TV and in the newspapers who, without knowing the language or much Balkan history, could peek into the heart of every living and long dead Serb, and in a few sentences explain to the American people what these strange folk were collectively feeling and thinking. It would be very bizarre if I did not get annoyed. They all claimed, for instance, that the age-old dream of Serbs was Greater Serbia. Well, in my entire life, with all the Serbs I have known, from every imaginable part of the political spectrum and so forth, I never heard a single one of them speak of Greater Serbia. I asked

Serbian friends whether they had ever heard anyone utter the phrase, and they told me that they had not.

Writing in 1997, on the process by which former Yugoslavia broke up, you stood against attempts to explain the tragedies from ethnic or cultural causes, preferring to point to "men who were the product of fifty years of Communism" as the root of the evils. I have every sympathy for the impatience you expressed in that article, 'Unfashionable Victims', with facile and fickle outsider views of former Yugoslavia, and I have precious little sympathy with the truthless and oppressive regimes that existed in the Communist world and have sometimes filled the vacuums it has left. Even so, I still feel in need of a little convincing. You provided only a little in your article. A satisfactory answer would of course be longer than this book; but can you say in more detail why you shift the focus in accounting for the Yugoslavian tragedies?

There were a few pieces in *The New Republic* and *The New York Times* during the NATO bombing which argued that Serbs were collectively guilty and deserved to be punished indiscriminately. Why? Because violence and ethnic cleansing is intrinsic to their culture and their history – in fact, it's in their genes. It was a racist argument that would have brought tears of joy to every Nazi ideologue. Of course, if one looks at any ethnic group closely, one finds that they've done many awful things in their past. In the Balkans, the peoples that historically survived did so by slaughtering countless now-forgotten tribes. It's not any different elsewhere in the world. My argument was that a fanatical, corrupt and evil minority can make hell for everyone. Sure, at some point, when the masses fall in behind and follow, there's collective madness, but that's not unusual: nationalism and civil war bring out the worst in every ethnic group. If one doesn't blame individuals, one ends up by dividing humanity into the eternally innocent and the eternally guilty, the way historian John Keegan did in *The Daily Telegraph*. He explained that "This war belongs within the much larger spectrum of a far older conflict between settled, creative productive Westerners and predatory, destructive Orientals." According to him, "A harsh, instantaneous attack may be the response most likely to impress the Islamic mind." He sounds like every fascist in Croatia and Serbia.

Is the political reality of the day a subject only for prose? I'm slightly perplexed, when I read your 1984 essay, 'Notes on Poetry and History', to find you vexed by poets who write of Nature or themselves but not

about "their executioners", poets for whom "history does not exist".
Agreed; but then, what is history but the political reality of today shifted
by time into yesterday? I can see that writing of the day's political affairs
in poems would run counter to your conviction that the poem finds its
own way, and I can see that making a headline or poster out of what
ought to be art could be unsatisfactory. But do you have a general an-
tipathy to political poetry?

Programmatic political poetry is what I am against. One may agree one
hundred percent with what the poems says, but it is still usually bad poetry. My point was that there is something monstrous about poetry that
never notices the world we live in. Okay, there are exceptions, poets
with their heads deep in the sand that I like very much. Still, it drives me
nuts to read dozens of new books and find no hint of human suffering. I
think: "Come on, boys and girls, all poets are narcissists, but you are
overdoing it and it's kind of embarrassing."

I think many of my poems can be called "political", although I do not sit
down with the intention of writing one. I just can't help noticing things. I
see some derelict sprawled half-dead on the sidewalk and I'm supposed
to forget about him? Even current political affairs come in – and why not?
We are not only the largest economy in the world, we are also competing
for the top spot when it comes to crooks and liars in public life.

Hans Magnus Enzensberger, to name only one example who springs to
mind, because of his connection with you, has published political com-
mentary of real distinction. Other writers (from Malraux to Havel to Vargas
Llosa, for instance) have actually entered political life, whether success-
fully or no. Speaking personally but also generically, how much value do
you think an active engagement with political debate, or even with po-
litical events, can have for the life of a writer?

It depends on the writer, of course. There are few of us as lucid as Hans
Magnus has been. The political engagement of most writers in the Balkans has been disastrous. One day they were Communist international-
ists, the next day they were enriching the vocabulary of exclusion and
hatred for their tribe. Not many among them could resist nationalism. In
fact, some of them are as guilty as the war criminals locked up in The
Hague. In the United States no one asks writers any political questions,
so there's no opportunity to make an ass of oneself. I don't believe it, nor
do I think writers as a group are smarter about politics than the rest of the
population.

The poem 'History' in Unending Blues, *and 'Marching Music' in* The Book of Gods and Devils, *and 'Frightening Toys' in the same collection, or 'Documentary' in* A Wedding in Hell, *all read like a blueprint for historical fatalism. People will be shot, tortured, die of hunger, and women will cry, and some dumb cluck will mouth a commentary on TV. Now, it may be that five hundred years of peace and harmony produce no better than the cuckoo clock, but still, given the choice, I'd take the peace and harmony over the torture and starvation. And I'd think it worth doing something for. Do you stand by the fatalism?*

I don't see it as fatalism. It's just the way things are. I've no objection to peace and harmony and am willing to work for it, but let's not delude ourselves. There are people in power in the United States who love a war now and then. Why do you think we have been breaking every international weapons treaty lately? So we can make a lot of weapons and continue to be the world's biggest merchant of arms. You obviously haven't been reading our strategic geniuses in Washington. They are always recommending sending a few missiles here and there to keep everybody in line. As the world's sole superpower, we need to flex our muscles from time to time. That kind of talk is not conducive to serenity even though they keep telling us that in our future war not a single one of our soldiers will die. As in Serbia, they'll just drops bombs from a great height and we'll sit in front of our TVs, sipping beer, eating pretzels, and watching as our enemies go up in flames.

Has history ended?

Only for stupid academics. As a writer I know said, "You can count on history creating another monster to harvest the millions." I agree completely. What are we going to do with all these guns we have? Use them as back-scratchers?

Asking you questions about the political dimension of a writer's life leaves me feeling I'm moving us back to the golden age of commitment, the Fifties or Sixties, or even the Thirties, some time when these questions appeared the be-all and end-all of a writer's identity. And plainly you're not a writer who'll sit comfortably in such a box. But then, I often have the impression that you have many readers (practising poets among them) who would do anything rather than read you in a framework of historical or political reality – as if the grotesquerie in your writing came out of nowhere and could be read in isolation from the world. How do you respond when you encounter naïve readings of your poetry?

Very true. They think of me as a Surrealist, a comic poet, a philosophical poet and even a mystic without realising that my poems are obsessed with the misery and horrors of the world. I agree with Dostoyevsky. As long as a single child suffers, to hell with your church and your civilisation. I have a tragic view but I can't say it has been noticed much. Perhaps because I joke around? As Jim Tate says, "It's a tragic story, but that's what's so funny."

As for that absence of historical sense in my readers – that's an American thing. History is bunk, etc. My students know next to nothing about the Vietnam War, not to mention all the other periods and issues in our history. So you can say, I'm a poet haunted by history writing in a country which long ago replaced history with utopia.

Thinking about your poetic temperament, as you've shown it in your poetry and prose and in the course of this interview, I might think (for example) of Coleridge's account of the poet "described in ideal perfection", in the fourteenth chapter of the Biographia Literaria. *For Coleridge, the poet balances or reconciles "the idea, with the image; the individual, with the representative; the sense of novelty and freshness, with old and familiar objects; a more than usual state of emotion, with more than usual order", and so forth. This, to my understanding, is what you do in your writing. It's interesting, though, that you prefer to claim (and have done so in this interview, in your answers to my questions about the object poems, restaurant settings, and key words) that you are all for the image, the individual, the object, rather than for the idea. Why this coyness from one so versed in philosophy?*

I agree with Coleridge completely. And I'm not being coy about ideas. I'm just wary of staying with abstractions. I don't trust thinking that has no basis in some particular reality. In that respect, I'm an heir to that empirical tradition in American poetry that goes back to Emerson and which includes such dissimilar poets as Frost, Stevens and W. C. Williams. My readings in philosophy come down to being alert to ideas lurking within a given experience. Once I have my foot in something concrete, I have no objection to speculating about its ramifications.

Isn't it in some sense true that your understanding of what poetry is for, what poetry is about, is best rendered in Arnold's words – that it is "a criticism of life"?

True enough, except that, like so many other nice definitions of poetry, it is also inadequate. There are so many other reasons one writes poetry. For example, the sheer pleasure of fooling around with language is what makes me go to my desk and open my notebook. I don't have any big plans. In fact, I have nothing specific in mind. Only a few words to play with. What happens later, after months and months of tinkering, is something else. In the process, I may surprise myself, and realise that I have something interesting to say.

There are three conceptions of good writing that were once among the religiously held tenets of literary culture in English and are now widely felt to be irrelevant to the practice of writing as understood by most contemporary poets and prose writers: Pope's "the sound must seem an echo to the sense", Swift's definition of a style as "proper words in proper places", and Arnold's that the pursuit of perfection is "the pursuit of sweetness and light". Could you give your own response to the ideas of writing represented by these views?

I understand what Pope means and that seems a worthy ideal to me. Swift's definition of style strikes me as obvious. Of course, the question arises, who decides? It had better be the poet and not some outside authority. As for Arnold, I have no idea what "pursuit of sweetness" may mean. "Light" makes more sense to me, as in lightness of touch. It's that seemingly effortless, airy quality we expect from a lyric poem and rarely get. I don't have any problem with that.

The present period has fewer difficulties subscribing to Wordsworth's view that "there neither is, nor can be, any essential difference between the language of prose and metrical composition." Why do you think this is?

Agreed. There can't be any essential difference, and yet ... Words in poetry end up by being different since so much depends on each word. Everything from the connotation of the word to its sound is exploited to the limit in a good poem. In poetry, the purpose of prosody is to make language stand still so that one may linger over each word and phrase. It has primarily a vertical (imaginative) dimension, while in prose – even in the most poetic kind of prose – it moves on. It's the same language, but used differently. In poetry you want to make a circle while in prose you want to go on telling an endless story.

A contemporary cultural preference, apparently shared in many parts of the world, is for poetry to be as free of thought as possible. Some, such as John Ashbery, have waged war on the concept of logical thought for poetological reasons; others have done so for ideological reasons, holding the concept to express a male dominance in received culture; still others seem simply to have developed an allergy to being preached at. Horace, who believed the arts should both delight and instruct, would presumably have had a hard time in an age so antipathetic to instruction. What is lost and what gained in this cultural shift?

Here's my recipe for turning poetry of the past into modern poetry. Remove from the poems every first stanza, the ones that announce that the poem will sing about this or that, and then remove the final stanza that sums it all up and leaves us with a wholesome message, a moral, or what have you. Yes, I gag at preaching in poems. It assumes that the reader is a half-wit who needs one last nudge to make certain he understood what he has just read. Sure, there are examples of genuine eloquence and wisdom in the long history of poetry, but in my view they are rare. Nothing much is lost by poets no longer telling their readers how to lead their lives. I have too great a respect for the intelligence and the imagination of these kind people to treat them like a bunch of idiots.

I remember a Belgian organiser of poetry readings explaining to me that all poetry in English was valueless because it had no understanding of "l'Autre". In the aphorisms in The Unemployed Fortune-Teller *you refer repeatedly to "the Other". Can you take the term out of the realm of capitalised indefinability and put a little everyday flesh on its poor otherworldly ineffable skeleton for me?*

The woman or some cat you like is an "Other" and so is a tree in your backyard. I'm not sure what the Belgian had in mind, but it sure sounds foolish. How about Shakespeare or Whitman? They had no understanding of "l'Autre"? What I had in mind is pretty obvious. We are not alone in the world. There are these "Others" we try to make sense of and communicate with and it's not easy. I've been married thirty-seven years, and my wife and I both understand and do not understand each other. The same goes for our parents and our children. As for the world out there, it's even worse. The "Other" is a metaphysical question for me, not a politically correct label.

Do you read much fiction? Who are the contemporary novelists you admire, and why?

I have, and I still do. I just re-read all of Saul Bellow's fiction for a piece I wrote on him. I love short stories, where I believe we Americans excel. Flannery O'Connor's, for instance. Come to think of it, I admire a number of Southern writers. Larry McMurtry, Barry Hannah, Eudora Welty, Cormack McCarthy come to mind. They have a great ear for language, and that to me is paradise. There are many others, of course. That man Sebald you've translated from German is magnificent, one of the most original writers to have come along in years.

Do you read contemporary philosophy? Given the manifold ways the self appears in your poetry, I'd be especially interested to know whether you've read Charles Taylor (Sources of the Self, The Ethics of Authenticity).

No, but I'd like to. There's just so much one ought to be reading. I read all the time and also do a lot of re-reading. As for contemporary philosophy: with a few exceptions, like Richard Rorty, I'm not very knowledgeable, and I regret that.

Which of your contemporaries in American poetry do you feel have a developed aesthetic that can sustain the interest of the over-forties?

Charles Wright, James Tate, Louise Glück and Mark Strand most definitely. There are others in our generation and the generation before us. We are already in our sixties, so after forty years or so of writing poems one ends up, both intentionally and unintentionally, by having some kind of an aesthetic and a world-view.

Which of the younger American poets (those who might not have crossed the Atlantic) would you recommend?

I can think of a few names – some of them not so young anymore – who ought to be known in England and elsewhere: Heather McHugh, Mekeel McBride, Mary Rueffle and Jonathan Aaron, for instance. There's no question that American poetry is worth reading. Alongside a lot of mediocre work, there are true originals like Russell Edson and Mark Jarman, who are simply terrific.

One of your best aphorisms is this: "To walk down a busy city block is a critical act." If you had to invent a city to suit your own critical preferences, which city that you know of would it most resemble? What changes would be top of your list?

My ideal city already exists. It is New York. I could use more sidewalk cafés in it, and some palm trees would be nice, but everything else I need is already there. After September 11, we even have ruins that make that part of town look like Europe in 1945. Sure, I like many other cities, but New York is the place where my imagination and intellect are at home. On and off, I've been living there and visiting regularly since 1954. It's changed a lot over the years, but I don't mind. I'm not surprised various religious fundamentalists and nationalists hate it. To see different races and ethnic groups work together and get along terrifies them since it goes against everything they believe. As we know, no Holy Warrior can endure the sight of a woman in a short skirt. The revenge of the small town bullies, village priests and provincial fascists has been the secret force behind so much recent history. They all dream of burning down the cities. What frightens them and makes them froth with hatred are the things I adore.

Auden's oft-parroted observation that "poetry makes nothing happen" is generally taken as a reminder of the ineffectuality of the art in the wider world. But it's always seemed to me that one might also emphasise the word "makes" to give a different meaning: that poetry is an enabling rather than a coercive influence. What might poetry make possible in the world – particularly, the world as changed by the events of September 11, 2001?

I heard from two booksellers that customers are buying serious books after September 11. I was teaching Whitman and Dickinson these last few weeks and my students told me that it did them good to read these poets. Great poetry deals with fundamental questions of life and death in a language that is memorable, that both moves us and makes us think. Suddenly, even familiar poems mean so much more to us. With their help, we see the world we live in with new eyes, and that's what we all need in these dreadful times.

Like other contributors to a London Review of Books *symposium on the events of September 11, you were critical of an American sense that tragedies would always happen elsewhere, and the notion (expressed by Milosz) that it might be possible to pass through history without suffering. Mary Beard, in a contribution to the same symposium that subsequently drew criticism, suggested that what "many people openly or privately think" is this: "World bullies, even if their heart is in the right place, will in the end pay the price." Does September 11 mark a final end to the sense of innocence enshrined in American culture?*

We all hope so. Losing our national innocence has become a big joke in America, since we seem to have lost it many times already, only to regain it. This time is different. You remember, answering an earlier question, I said that since the US was never bombed and didn't have the experience of seeing its cities in ruins, it had missed out on that aspect of twentieth century experience? No more. The rubble of the World Trade Centre towers and the surrounding buildings made even this Second World War child, who saw Belgrade and other European cities in ruin, physically ill. New York certainly will never be the same. For now, people have become much more thoughtful; their "priorities have changed", as they say. Everyone from the FBI down believes that there will be another terrorist attack soon, followed by many more years of such madness. So everyone's on edge. This is the sixth war in my life, but they don't get any easier. Despite my chronic pessimism, I had a vague hope, after the wars in former Yugoslavia ended, that I would have a peaceful old age. Clearly this is no longer on the cards for me and for millions of others.

△

The Secret Doctrine

Psst, psst, psst,
Is what the snow is saying
To the quiet woods,
With the night falling.

Something pressing,
That can't wait,
On a path that went nowhere,
Where I found myself

Overtaken by these flakes
With so much to confide.
The bare twigs pricked their ears –
Great God!

What did they say?
What did they say?
I went badgering
Every tree and bush.

Nearest Nameless

So damn familiar
Most of the time,
I don't even know you are here
My life,
My portion of eternity,

A little shiver,
As if the chill of the grave
Is already
Catching up with me –
No matter.

Descartes smelled
Witches burning
While he sat thinking
Of a truth so obvious
We keep failing to see it.

I never knew it either
Till today.
When I heard a bird shriek:
The cat is coming,
And I felt myself tremble.

Empty Barbershop

In pursuit of happiness, you may yet
Draw close to it momentarily
In one of these two leather-bound chairs
With the help of scissors and a comb,

Draped to the chin with a long white sheet,
While your head slips through
The invisible barber's greasy fingers
Making your hair stand up straight,

While he presses the razor to your throat,
Causing your eyes to pop open
As you discern in the mirror before you
The full length of the empty barbershop

With two vacant chairs and past them,
The street, commensurately empty,
Except for the pressed and blurred face
Of someone straining to look inside.

Simic Bibliography

COMPILED BY RYAN ROBERTS AND PHILIP HOY

While everything has been done to ensure the completeness and accuracy of this bibliography, the compilers can be sure that their efforts have not been entirely successful. The editors would therefore be pleased to hear from anyone who can identify omissions or errors, which it would be their hope to repair in future editions.

Primary Works

Poetry

Books

In English

What the Grass Says [with illustrations by Joan Abelson] (Kayak, Santa Cruz, 1967).
Somewhere among Us a Stone Is Taking Notes (Kayak, San Francisco, 1969).
Dismantling the Silence [with a note by Richard Howard] (Braziller, New York, 1971/Jonathan Cape, London, 1971).
White (New Rivers Press, New York, 1972) [limited to 1,300 copies, of which 300 have been bound in cloth and 1,000 in paper wraps; 30 of the hardbound edition are numbered and signed by Simic].
Return to a Place Lit by a Glass of Milk (Braziller, New York, 1974).
Biography and a Lament, Poems 1961-1967 (Bartholomew's Cobble, Hartford, Connecticut, 1976) [limited to 250 copies, of which 50 are numbered and signed by Simic].
Charon's Cosmology (Braziller, New York, 1977).
Classic Ballroom Dances (Braziller, New York, 1980).
White: A New Version (Logbridge-Rhodes Press, Durango, Colorado, 1980).
Austerities (Braziller, New York, 1982/Secker and Warburg, London, 1983).
Weather Forecast for Utopia and Vicinity, Poems 1967-1982 (Station Hill Press, Barrytown, New York, 1983).
Selected Poems, 1963-1983 (Braziller, New York, 1985/Secker and Warburg, London, 1986).
Unending Blues (Harcourt Brace Jovanovich, San Diego, California, 1986).
The World Doesn't End (Harcourt Brace Jovanovich, San Diego, California, 1989).
The Book of Gods and Devils (Harcourt Brace Jovanovich, San Diego, California, 1990).
Selected Poems, 1963-1983: Revised and Expanded (Braziller, New York, 1990).
Hotel Insomnia (Harcourt Brace Jovanovich, San Diego, California, 1992).
A Wedding in Hell (Harcourt Brace, New York, 1994).
Frightening Toys (Faber and Faber, London, 1995).
Walking the Black Cat (Harcourt Brace, New York, 1996).
Looking for Trouble (Faber and Faber, London, 1997).
Jackstraws (Harcourt Brace, New York, 1999/Faber and Faber, London, 1999).
Selected Early Poems (Braziller, New York, 1999).
Night Picnic (Harcourt, New York, 2001).

Forthcoming

The Voice at 3A.M.: Selected Later Poems (Harcourt, New York, 2003).

In Other Languages

Demantelement du Silence (Rougerie, Paris, 1979).
Een Plek Verlicht door een Glas Melk (Tabula, Amsterdam, 1983)
Izabrane Pesme 1965-1982 (Nolit, Belgrade, 1983).
Prognoza za Gradot Utopija so Okolinata (Misla, Skopje, 1984).

Pesme (Knjizevne Novine, Belgrade, 1989).
Svet se ne Zavrsava: Pesme u Prozi (Narodna Knjiga, Belgrade, 1990).
Avenija Amerika (KOB, Yugoslavia, 1992).
Madonny z Dorysowanna Szpickbródka (Wydawn, Poznan, 1992).
Een Hond met Vleugels: Gedichten (Meulenhoff, Amsterdam, 1993).
Ein Buch von Gottern und Feufeln (Hanser, Munich, 1993).
In den Beginne was de Radio (Meulenhoff, Amsterdam, 1993).
El Sueño del Alquimista (UNAM, Mexico City, 1994).
Hotel Nesanica (KOB, Yugoslavia, 1994).
Hjulet Snakkar Nar Det Gar (Samlaget, Oslo, 1995).
Le Livre des Dieux et des Demons (Circe, Paris, 1995).
Una Boda en el Infierno (Breve Fondo Editorial, Mexico City, 1996).
4 Frauenfelder Lyriktage [with Vreni Schwalder] (Verlag im Waldgut, Frauenfeld, 1997).
Hotel Insomnio (Nomadas, Oviedo, Spain, 1998).
El Mundo No Se Acaba y Otros Poemas (DVD Ediciones, Barcelona, 1999).
El Pollo Sin Cabeza (FEPV, Caracas, 1999).
Fabrika Sirocadi (Paideia, Belgrade, 1999).
Medici Groschengrab (Carl Hasner Verlag, Munich, 1999).
Grubelei im Rinsttein (Carl Hanser Verlag, Munich, 2000).
Totemismo Y Otros Poemas (Alcion Editora, Cordoba, Argentina, 2000).
Hotel Insomnia (Tiden Norsk Forlag, Oslo, 2001).
Il Mondo Non Finice (Donzelli, Roma, 2001).
Kasni Poziv (Okrovenje, Belgrade, 2001).
Hotel Insomnia (Adelphi, Milan, 2002).
Previsa de Tempo Para Utopia e Arredores (Assirio & Alvim, Lisbon, 2002).

PAMPHLETS, SPECIAL EDITIONS, BROADSIDES

Poem (Stonybrook Poetics Foundation, New York, 1968).
Three Poems, [Unicorn Folio Series, 2:4] (Unicorn Press, Santa Barbara, California, 1968) [limited to 350 copies; includes broadsides from several poets].
Aunt Lettuce, I Want to Look under Your Skirt (Wang Hui-Ming, 1971) [limited to a few proofs; reproduced in *The Land on the Tip of a Hair* (Wang Hui-Ming, 1972)].
Knife (Cottonwood Review, Lawrence, Kansas, 1972).
Further Adventures of Charles Simic [with illustration by William Lint] (Rook Press, Derry, Pennsylvania, 1975) [limited to 300 copies, numbered and signed by Lint and Simic].
Happy End [with *Fear of Death* by John Ashbery] (Library of Congress, Washington D.C., 1975).
Poem (International Poetry Forum, Pittsburgh, Pennsylvania, 1975).
Brooms (Edge Press, Barry, Wales, 1978) [limited to 300 copies].
School for Dark Thoughts (Charles Seluzicki, Baltimore, Maryland, 1978) [limited to 235 copies signed by Simic; printed by Banyan Press on Weimar papers and sewn into Roma coversheets].
The Message Is Confined to the Species (Nadja, New York, 1979) [limited to 100 copies, with 26 lettered copies printed as holiday greeting].
They Forage at Night (Nadja, New York, 1980) [limited to 74 numbered and 26 lettered copies signed by Simic].
Interlude [with artwork by Sarah Chamberlain] (Charles Seluzicki, Salem, Oregon, 1981) [limited to 135 copies signed by Chamberlain and Simic].
Shaving at Night: Poems [with illustrations by Helen Siegl] (Meadow Press, San Francisco, California, 1982) [limited to 200 copies signed by Siegl and Simic].
The Chicken Without a Head: A New Version (Trace Editions, Portland, Oregon, 1983) [limited to 500 copies].
Watch Repair [with illustrations by Mare Blocker] (M. Kimberley Press, Seattle, Washington, 1987) [signed, limited edition of 25 copies].
Nine Poems: A Childhood Story (Exact Change, Cambridge, Massachussetts, 1989) [limited to 500 copies].
Pyramids and Sphinxes (Nadja, New York, 1989) [limited to 74 numbered and 26 lettered copies].
Evening Walk [with woodcuts by Gary Young] (Greenhouse Review Press, Santa Cruz, California, 1991)

[limited to 90 copies].

Displaced Person (New Directions, New York, 1995) [signed, limited edition of 150 copies].

'The Number of Fools', *Writing for Bernadette*, edited by William Corbett and Gizzi, Michael (The Figures, Great Barrington, Massachusetts, 1995) [contains broadsides from 25 contributors in an edition of 26 lettered copies, each signed by the author with the exception of the one by James Schuyler].

On the Music of the Spheres [with photographs by Linda Connor] (Grenfell Press, New York, 1996); also published as 'Night Sky' in *Orphan Factory* (see under Primary Works/Prose/Books/In English).

Wendy's Pinball: Poems [with images by Wendy Mark] (Glenn Horowitz, East Hampton, New York, 1996).

In the Library [with engravings by Barry Moser] (Firefly Press, Concord, New Hampshire, 1997) [limited to 1,100 copies for private distribution by the Friends of the University of New Hampshire Library; of these, 150 copies were printed on Rives heavyweight paper and signed by Moser and Simic (excerpt from *The Book of Gods and Devils* {see under Primary Works/Poetry/Books/In English})].

The Pieces of the Clock Lie Scattered [with illustrations by Holly Brown] (Brown, Syracuse, New York, 1997) [consists of five etchings inspired by the poetry of Simic; limited to 10 copies signed by Brown and one artist proof].

Against Winter [with illustration by R.P. Hale] (William B. Ewert, Concord, New Hampshire, 1998) [limited to 450 copies; 40 copies numbered and signed by Hale and Simic (excerpt from *Walking the Black Cat* {see under Primary Works/Poetry/Books/In English})].

Small Feast: Poems (William B. Ewert, Concord, New Hampshire, 1998) [limited to 55 copies signed by Simic].

Sweet Tooth [with illustration by R. P. Hale] (William B. Ewert, Concord, New Hampshire, 1999) [limited to 250 copies; 40 copies numbered and signed by Hale and Simic].

The Improbable (William Corbett, 2000) [a collection of broadsides endowing the first annual Pressed Wafer Lifetime Achievement Award; limited to 26 copies lettered A-Z].

INDEX OF POEMS APPEARING IN SIMIC'S ENGLISH-LANGUAGE COLLECTIONS

GS = *What the Grass Says* (1967)

STN = *Somewhere among Us a Stone Is Taking Notes* (1969)

DS = *Dismantling the Silence* (1971)

Wh = *White* (1972)

RP = *Return to a Place Lit by a Glass of Milk* (1974)

BL = *Biography and a Lament, Poems 1961-1967* (1976)

CC = *Charon's Cosmology* (1977)

CB = *Classic Ballroom Dances* (1980)

TFN = *They Forage at Night* (1980).

WhNV = *White: A New Version* (1980)

Au = *Austerities* (1982; 1983)

WF = *Weather Forecast for Utopia and Vicinity, Poems 1967-1982* (1983)

SP = *Selected Poems, 1963-1983* (1985; 1986)

UB = *Unending Blues* (1986)

PS = *Pyramids and Sphinxes* (1989)

WDE = *The World Doesn't End* (1989)

GD = *The Book of Gods and Devils* (1990)

SPR = *Selected Poems, 1963-1983: Revised and Expanded* (1990)

HI = *Hotel Insomnia* (1992)

WH = *A Wedding in Hell* (1994)

FT = *Frightening Toys* (1995)

WBC = *Walking the Black Cat* (1996)

LT = *Looking for Trouble* (1997)

J = *Jackstraws* (1999)

SEP = *Selected Early Poems* (1999)

NP = *Night Picnic* (2001)

72

'Gallows Etiquette'. SPR: 192; SEP: 208.
'Gas Station'. NP: 78.
'George Simic'. RP: 43.
'Ghost stories written ...'. WDE: 13.
'Ghosts'. WBC: 30; LT: 91.
'Gospel'. WDE: 50.
'Gospel Hour'. SEP: 216.
'Grand Theatrics'. NP: 48.
'Grandmother Logic'. WF: 24.
'Gravity'. WF: 5; SPR: 180; SEP: 188.
'Gravity Plus Something Else'. BL: [11].
'Great Infirmities'. CB: 19; SP: 128; SPR: 144; SEP: 146.
'Green Lampshade'. CB: 25.
'Grim Contingencies'. WH: 35.
'Grocery'. CB: 51; SP: 140; SPR: 164; SEP: 168.
'Guardian Angel'. Au: 52.
'Happiness'. WH: 33.
'Happy End'. CC: 21; SP: 102; SPR: 115; SEP: 114.
'Harsh Climate'. CB: 54; SP: 142; SPR: 166; LT: 46; SEP: 171.
'Haunted Mind'. WH: 9.
'Have You Met Miss Jones?'. WBC: 24; LT: 87.
'He calls one dog Rimbaud ...'. WDE: 28; FT: 30.
'He had mixed up the characters ...'. WDE: 71; FT: 41.
'He held the Beast ...'. WDE: 11.
'Head of a Doll'. J: 64.
'Hearing Steps'. GS: [22]; DS: 30.
'Heights of Folly'. GD: 45.
'Help Wanted'. CC: 12; SP: 99; SPR: 112; LT: 34; SEP: 111.
'Henri Rousseau's Bed'. UB: 45.
'Heroic Moment'. WH: 30.
'History Book'. WF: 20; SPR: 179; SEP: 182.
'History Lesson'. WDE: 21; FT: 28.
'History' ['On a gray evening']. Au: 13; SP: 166; SPR: 205; SEP: 224.
'History' ['Men and Women with kick-me signs on their backs']. UB: 15.
'Hit-Parade'. STN: 40.
'Hoarder of Tragedy'. WH: 53.
'Homecoming'. BL: [5].
'Home'. WF: 6.
'Hot Night'. WBC: 76.
'Hotel Insomnia'. HI: 12; FT: 76.
'Hotel Starry Sky'. HI: 29; FT: 86.
'House of Horrors'. J: 62.
'House'. STN: 49.
'How to Psalmodise'. STN: 34.
'Hunger'. STN: 37; DS: 15.
'Hurricane Season'. Au: 31; SP: 165; SPR: 201; SEP: 219.
'I am the last Napoleonic soldier ...'. WDE: 9; FT: 26.
'I Climbed a Tree to Make Sure'. NP: 44.
'I knew a night owl ...'. WDE: 65.
'I Played in the Smallest Theatres ...'. WDE: 16.
'I was stolen by the gypsies ...'. WDE: 5; FT: 25.
'I've Had My Little Stroll'. NP: 85.
'Immortal Prankster'. SEP: 159.
'Imported Novelties'. WH: 71; LT: 80.

'In a forest of question marks ...'. WDE: 26; FT: 29.
'In a Forest of Whispers'. WBC: 59; LT: 103.
'In Ecstasy of Surrender'. WH: 50.
'In Midsummer Quiet'. WF: 37; SP: 159; SPR: 193; LT: 48; SEP: 209.
'In Solitary'. NP: 58.
'In Strange Cities'. WH: 62.
'In the Alley'. UB: 28; FT: 11.
'In the Courtroom'. NP: 75.
'In the fourth year ...'. WDE: 14.
'In the Library'. GD: 64.
'In the Night'. FT: 89.
'In the Rathole'. NP: 59.
'In the Street'. J: 39.
'In Times of Widespread Evil'. UB: 32.
'Independent Testimony'. WF: 41.
'Inheritance'. Au: 20; SP: 171; SPR: 210; SEP: 230.
'Insomniacs' Debating Society'. J: 57.
'Interlude'. Au: 48; SP: 180; SPR: 221; SEP: 246.
'Interrogating Mr. Worm'. NP: 80.
'Invention of a Color'. DS: 78.
'Invention of Nothing'. DS: 79; SP: 42; SPR: 48; SEP: 48.
'Invention of the Hat'. DS: 79.
'Invention of the Invisible'. DS: 76.
'Invention of the Knife'. DS: 76.
'Invention of the Place'. DS: 77.
'It was the epoch of the masters ...'. WDE: 12; FT: 27.
'It's a store ...'. WDE: 6.
'Jackstraws' ['The penny arcade silhouettes']. Au: 49.
'Jackstraws' ['My shadow and your shadow on the wall']. J: 46.
'Jar of Fireflies'. NP: 51.
'Kitchen Helper'. WBC: 47.
'Knife'. STN: 16; DS: 56; SP: 31; SPR: 36; SEP: 35.
'Last Supper'. STN: 41; DS: 27.
'Late'. Au: 22.
'Late Arrival'. WH: 4; LT: 60.
'Late Call'. WBC: 67; LT: 105.
'Late Train'. WBC: 65.
'Le Beau Monde'. GD: 19; FT: 54.
'Le Dame e i Cavalieri'. WBC: 10.
'Leaves'. WH: 46.
'Leaving an Unknown City'. NP: 33.
'Like Whippoorwills'. CB: 63.
'Little Prophet'. WH: 76.
'Little Unwritten Book'. WBC: 22.
'Live at Club Revolution'. J: 12.
'Lone Tree'. WBC: 60.
'Lost Glove'. HI: 50; FT: 94.
'Lots of people around here ...'. WDE: 63; FT: 38.
'Love Flea'. WH: 43; LT: 70.
'Love Poem'. J: 42.
'Love Worker'. HI: 53.
'Lover of endless ...'. WDE: 19.
'M.'. WDE: 53; FT: 35.
'Mad Business'. WH: 27.
'Madame Thebes'. WH: 15; LT: 64.
'Madge Put On Your Teakettle'. NP: 37.
'Madonnas Touched Up with a Goatee'. Au: 42; SP: 182; SPR: 223; LT: 55; as 'Madonnas Touched

'Poem' ['Every morning I forget how it is.']. GS: [46]; DS: 5; SP: 26; SPR: 28; LT: 3; SEP: 27.

'Poem' ['My father writes all day, all night:']. STN: 44; CC: 8; SP: 97; SPR: 110; SEP: 109.

'Poem' ['My little girl sings at night']. GS: [21].

'Poem' ['The enigma of the invisible is the enigma']. RP: 25.

'Poem' ['The flies go to bless the spiders']. GS: [25].

'Poem' ['Those happy days when I climbed']. HI: 33.

'Police dogs ...'. WDE: 56.

'Poor Little Devil'. J: 18.

'Popular Mechanics'. UB: 26; FT: 10.

'Pornographer's Psalm'. RP: 39.

'Position without a Magnitude'. CC: 47; SP: 115; SPR: 132; SEP: 135.

'Poverty'. GS: [41].

'Prayer'. WH: 68; LT: 79.

'Primer'. CB: 15; SP: 119; SPR: 135; SEP: 137.

'Prison Guards Silhouetted Against the Sky'. J: 43.

'Prison'. WF: 42; SEP: 205.

'Private Eye'. J: 8.

'Prodigy'. CB: 21; SP: 122; SPR: 138; LT: 38; SEP: 140.

'Progress Report'. CC: 15; SEP: 170.

'Promises of Leniency and Forgiveness'. UB: 52.

'Psalm' ['Old ones to the side']. STN: 35; DS: 32; SP: 24; SPR: 26; SEP: 25.

'Psalm' ['You've been a long time making up your mind']. WH: 58; LT: 75.

'Punch Minus Judy'. Au: 54; SEP: 234.

'Pyramids and Sphinxes'. PS: unnumbered; HI: 62; FT: 98.

'Quick Eats'. HI: 34.

'Raskolnikov'. WH: 23.

'Reading History'. WH: 55; LT: 73.

'Relaxing in a Madhouse'. WBC: 3.

'Religious Miniatures'. WF: 29.

'Return to a Place Lit by a Glass of Milk'. RP: 61.

'Rivers'. GS: [8].

'Roach Motel'. WBC: 4.

'Roadside Stand'. NP: 46.

'Roll Call'. CB: 18.

'Romantic Landscape'. WH: 66; LT: 78.

'Romantic Sonnet'. HI: 54.

'Rosalia'. Au: 34; SP: 172; SPR: 211.

'Rough Outline'. Au: 21; SP: 167; SPR: 206; SEP: 225.

'Rural Delivery'. Au: 24; SPR: 224; SEP: 249.

'Scaliger turns deadly pale ...'. WDE: 4; FT: 24.

'School for Dark Thoughts'. CB: 16; SP: 120; SPR: 136; SEP: 138.

'School for Visionaries'. J: 51.

'Second Avenue Winter'. RP: 9.

'Sewing Machine'. WF: 48; SEP: 187.

'Shadow Publishing Company'. WBC: 11.

'Shaving at Night'. Au: 25; SPR: 217; SEP: 241.

'Shaving'. WH: 73.

'She's pressing me ...'. WDE: 7.

'Shelley'. GD: 10; FT: 50.

'Ship of Fools'. J: 33.

'Shirt'. CB: 35; SP: 127; SPR: 143; LT: 42; SEP: 145.

'Shortcut'. SEP: 197.

'Silent Child'. UB: 47.

'Sinister Company'. WH: 8.

'Slaughterhouse Flies'. WBC: 50; LT: 100.

'Sleep'. GS: [43]; DS: 19; SEP: 24.

'Sleepwalkers'. NP: 31.

'Small Wonders'. SEP: 235.

'Solitude' ['There now, where the first crumb']. RP: 14; SP: 67; SPR: 75; LT: 15; SEP: 76.

'Solitude' ['The old pilgrims brought it']. STN: 32.

'Solving the Riddle'. RP: 28; SP: 59; SPR: 67; SEP: 66.

'Some Nights'. HI: 56.

'Someone shuffles by my door ...'. WDE: 72; FT: 42.

'Song' ['In her widow's purse']. CC: 11.

'Song' ['There's a house on the tip of a branch']. RP: 10.

'Soup'. RP: 62.

'Sparrow'. GS: [28].

'Species'. CC: 31.

'Speck-Sized Screaming Head'. J: 4.

'Spider'. STN: 46; DS: 12.

'Spoon'. STN: 15; DS: 54; SP: 30; SPR: 35; SEP: 34 [also published as 'The Spoon'].

'Spoons with Realistic Dead Flies on Them'. Au: 14; SPR: 204; SEP: 223.

'Spring'. HI: 51.

'Squinting Suspiciously'. WBC: 72.

'St. George and the Dragon'. J: 21.

'St. Thomas Aquinas'. GD: 4; FT: 44.

'Stand-In'. NP: 28.

'Stealing from Mice'. WF: 17.

'Stone inside a Stone'. STN: 25; DS: 60.

'Stone'. GS: [11]; DS: 59; SP: 35; SPR: 40; LT: 8; SEP: 39.

'Story of My Luck'. HI: 52.

'Street of Jewelers'. NP: 5.

'Street Scene'. HI: 58; FT: 96.

'Streets Paved with Gold'. J: 19.

'Strictly Bucolic'. Au: 33; SP: 168; SPR: 207; LT: 49; SEP: 226.

'Strictly for Posterity'. RP: 42.

'Strong Boy'. UB: 35.

'Stub of a Red Pencil'. HI: 9; FT: 73.

'Suffering'. BL: [13].

'Summa Theologica'. WF: 30.

'Summer in the Country'. NP: 43.

'Summer Morning'. GS: [5]; DS: 8; SPR: 29; SEP: 28.

'Sunday Papers'. NP: 14.

'Sunset's Coloring Book'. WBC: 58; LT: 102.

'Sweet Tooth'. NP: 17.

'Table'. STN: 14; DS: 51.

'Taking a Breather'. J: 26.

'Talking to Little Birdies'. WBC: 13.

'Talking to the Ceiling'. J: 74.

'Tapestry'. STN: 11; DS: 31; SP: 14; SPR: 16; LT: 2; SEP: 13.

'Tattooed City'. WH: 6; LT: 61.

'Thanksgiving'. WF: 27.

'That Straightlaced Christian Thing between Her Legs'. RP: 54.

'The Absent Spider'. HI: 63.

'The Altar'. NP: 25.

BOOKS

Fire Gardens: Selected Poems, 1956-1969, by Ivan V. Lalic, with C.W. Truesdale, and drawings by Zivotin Turinski (New Rivers Press, New York, 1970) [limited to 600 copies].

Four Yugoslav Poets: Ivan V. Lalic, Branko Miljkovic, Milorad Pavic, Ljubomir Simovic (Lillabulero Press, Northwood Narrows, New Hampshire, 1970).

The Poetry of Surrealism: An Anthology, with introduction by Michael Benedikt (Little, Brown and Company, Boston and Toronto, 1974) [includes translations by Simic].

Three Slavic Poets: Joseph Brodsky, Tymotensz Karpowicz, Djordje Nikolic, edited by John Rezek (Elpenor Books, Chicago, 1975) [limited to 500 copies; Simic translates Nikolic's poems 'Road', 'Love Poem', and 'Grave'].

Another Republic: 17 European and South American Writers, edited by Charles Simic and Mark Strand (Ecco Press, Hopewell, New Jersey, 1976).

Contemporary Yugoslav Poetry, edited by Vasa D. Mihailovich (University of Iowa Press, Iowa City, 1977) [includes translations by Simic].

Key to Dreams According to Djordje, by Djordje Nikolic (Elpenor Books, Chicago, 1978) [no limitation, but 30 copies are lettered in Serbian Cyrillic and signed by Simic].

Homage to the Lame Wolf: Selected Poems, 1956-1975, by Vasko Popa, with an introduction by Simic [Field Translation Series, 2] (Oberlin College, Oberlin, Ohio, 1979).

Atlantis: Selected Poems 1953-1982, by Slavko Mihalic, with Peter Kastmiler (Greenfield Review Press, Greenfield Center, New York, 1983).

Selected Poems of Tomaz Šalamun, with an introduction by Robert Hass (Ecco Press, Hopewell, New Jersey, 1988).

Roll Call of Mirrors: Selected Poems of Ivan V. Lalic, with an introduction by Simic (Wesleyan University Press, Middletown, Connecticut, 1988).

Some Other Wine and Light, by Aleksandar Ristovic [Foreword by Simic] (Charioteer Press, Washington D.C., 1989) ['To a Fool', 'Old Motif', 'Landscape with Snow', 'Happiness', and 'Out in the Open'; also published in *Paris Review,* 31:110, Spring 1989: 168-172].

The Bandit Wind, by Slavko Janevski (Dryad Press, Takoma Park, Maryland, 1991).

The Horse Has Six Legs: An Anthology of Serbian Poetry (Graywolf Press, St Paul, Minnesota, 1992).

Night Mail, by Novica Tadic, [Field Translation Series, 19] (Oberlin College Press, Oberlin, Ohio, 1992).

Faceless Men and Other Macedonian Stories, with Jeffrey Folks and Milne Holton (Forest Books, London/ Boston, 1992).

Scar on the Stone: Contemporary Poetry from Bosnia, edited by Chris Agee (Bloodaxe Books, Newcastle upon Tyne, 1998) [Simic translates Izet Sarajlic, Dara Sekulic, and Hamdija Demirovic].

Devil's Lunch, by Aleksandar Ristovic (Faber and Faber, London, 1999).

Horace: The Odes, edited by J. D. McClatchy (Princeton University Press, Princeton, New Jersey, 2002) [Simic translates I.6, II.15, and III.11].

PAMPHLETS, LIMITED EDITIONS, BROADSIDES

Four Yugoslav Poets: Ivan V. Lalic, Branko Miljkovic, Milorad Pavic, Ljubomir Simovic (Lillabulero Press, Northwood Narrows, New Hampshire, 1970).

The Little Box, by Vasko Popa (Charioteer Press, Washington D.C., 1970) [limited to 350 copies].

Give Me Back My Rags, by Vasko Popa (Trace Editions, Portland, Oregon, 1985) [limited to 600 copies in portfolio, of which 75 copies are numbered and signed, and 26 copies are lettered and signed and contain a holograph poem by Simic].

EDITIONS AND SELECTIONS BY SIMIC

Campion, Thomas, *The Essential Campion,* selected and introduced by Simic [The Essential Poets Series, 7] (Ecco Press, Hopewell, New Jersey, 1988).

Rosser, J. Allyn, *Bright Moves,* selected and introduced by Simic (Northeastern University Press, Boston, Massuchusetts, 1990) (see also under Primary Works/Prose/Prefaces, Introductions, Forewords).

The Best American Poetry, 1992, edited by Simic and David Lehman (Macmillan, New York, 1992).
Tall, Deborah, Summons: Poems, selected by Simic (Sarabande Books, Louisville, Kentucky, 2000).
Šalamun, Tomaz, Feast (Harcourt, New York/London, 2000).

PROSE

BOOKS

IN ENGLISH

The Uncertain Certainty: Interviews, Essays, and Notes on Poetry (University of Michigan Press, Ann Arbor, 1985): I. Interviews: 'With Crazy Horse', 3-10; 'With Wayne Dodd and Stanley Plumly', 11-26; 'With George Starbuck', 27-45; 'With Rod Steier', 46-50; 'With Students at Interlochen School', 51-57; 'With Rick Jackson and Michael Panori', 58-67; 'With Sherod Santos', 68-79; II. Essays, Introductions, Notes: 'Negative Capability and Its Children', 83-91; 'Vasko Popa', 92-95; 'A Retired School Teacher in Galoshes', 96; 'Péret', 97-100; 'The Partial Explanation', 101-104; 'Images and "Images"', 105-107; 'A Clear and Open Place', 108-109; 'Composition', 110-112; 'Some Thoughts About the Line', 113-114; 'Streets Strewn with Garbage, 115-117; 'The Infinitely Forked Mother Tongue', 118-119; 'Classic Ballroom Dances', 120-123; 'Notes on Poetry and History', 124-128.
Wonderful Words, Silent Truth: Essays on Poetry and a Memoir (University of Michigan Press, Ann Arbor, 1990): 'Why I Like Certain Poems More Than Others', 1-2; 'In the Beginning...', 3-53; 'Reading Philosophy at Night'; 54-61; 'Notes on Poetry and Philosophy', 62-68; 'Chinese Boxes and Puppet Theaters', 69-71; 'Visionaries and Anti-Visionaries', 72-81; 'Caballero Solo', 82-84; 'Wonderful Words, Silent Truth', 85-95; 'Thomas Campion', 96-100; 'Ivan V. Lalic', 101-107; 'Serbian Heroic Ballads', 108-112; 'Introduction to the Poetry of Aleksandar Ristovic', 113-116; 'Art Hodes',117-119; 'Notes on Bata Mihailovitch's Paintings', 120-125; 'William Stafford's "At the Bomb Testing Site"',126-128.
Dime-Store Alchemy: The Art of Joseph Cornell (Ecco Press, Hopewell, New Jersey, 1992).
The Unemployed Fortune-Teller: Essays and Memoirs (University of Michigan Press, Ann Arbor, 1994): 'The Flute Player in the Pit',1-5; 'Food and Happiness', 6-12; 'The Little Venus of the Eskimos', 13-18; 'Fried Sausage', 19-21; 'Bicycle Thieves', 22-25; 'Lady Be Good', 26-33; 'Elegy in a Spider's Web', 34-39; 'Novica Tadic', 40-42; 'Shop, Le Bacarès', 43-45; 'No Cure for the Blues', 46-52; 'Poetry Is the Present', 53-57; 'The Necessity of Poetry', 58-74; 'Luneville Diary (December 1, 1962—March 1, 1963)', 75-97; 'Red Knight', 98-100. 'The Minotaur Loves His Labyrinth', 101-114; 'Sigmund Abeles', 115-117; 'Ales Debeljak', 118-119; 'Don't Squeeze the Tomatoes!', 120-127.
Orphan Factory (University of Michigan Press, Ann Arbor, 1998): 'New York Days, 1958-1964', 1-15; 'Charles the Obscure'; 16-21; 'Orphan Factory', 22-27; 'In Praise of Invective', 28-31; 'The Trouble with Poetry', 32-35; 'Poetry and Experience', 36-39; 'Cut the Comedy', 40-42; 'Poets' Notebooks', 43-45; 'The Poetry of Village Idiots', 46-47; 'My Insomnia and I', 48-49; 'Fearful Paradise', 50-54; 'My Unwritten Books', 55-62; 'Time Channel', 63-64; 'Dinner at Uncle Boris', 65-69; 'On Dreams', 70-71; 'Jane Kenyon', 72-73; 'Ingeborg Bachmann', 74-77; 'Don Quixote Charging a Pineapple', 78-83; 'Holly Wright's Photographs of Hands', 84-86; 'Open Wounds', 87-89; 'Assembly Required', 90-98; 'Night Sky', 99-114; 'Contributor's Note', 115.
A Fly in the Soup (University of Michigan Press, Ann Arbor, 2000).

FORTHCOMING

Metaphysician in the Dark (University of Michigan Press, Ann Arbor, 2003)

IN OTHER LANGUAGES

Nezaposleni vidovcak: eseji i secaya [Unemployed Fortune-Teller] (KOV/Mentor, Vršak/Panchevo, 1995).
Alquimia de tendajón: el arte de Joseph Cornell (Universidad Nacional Autónoma de México, Mexico, 1996).
Die Fliege in der Suppe (Hanser, Munich, 1997).

80

BOOKS AND CATALOGUES CONTRIBUTED TO

The Young American Poets, edited by Paul Carroll (Follett, Chicago/New York, 1968).

Five Blind Men: Poems by Dan Gerber, Jim Harrison, George Quasha, J.D. Reed and Charlie Simic (Sumac Press, Freemont, Michigan, 1969).

'The Partial Explanation', *Fifty Contemporary Poets*, edited by Alberta T. Turner (Longman, Boston, 1977); also published in *The Uncertain Certainty* (see under Primary Works/Prose/Books/In English).

Focus 101, edited by La Verne Harrell Clark (Heidelberg Graphics, Chico, California, 1979).

'Negative Capability and Its Children', *Claims for Poetry*, edited by Donald Hall (University of Michigan Press, Ann Arbor, 1982): 399-406; also published in *Antaeus*; also published in *The Uncertain Certainty* (see under Primary Works/Prose/Books/In English).

'Classic Ballroom Dances', *Forty Five Contemporary Poets*, edited by Alberta T. Turner (Longman, Boston, 1985); also published in *The Uncertain Certainty* (see under Primary Works/Prose/Books/In English).

'In the Beginning ...', *Contemporary Authors: Autobiography Series*, volume 4 (Gale Research, Detroit, 1986): 267-284; also published in *Antaeus* (see under Primary Works/Prose/Magazine Articles, Reviews, etc); also published in *Wonderful Words, Silent Truth* (see under Primary Works/Prose/Books/In English).

'The Infinitely Forked Mother Tongue', *Translations: Experiments in Reading, A-C*, edited by Don Wellman, Cola Franzen, and Irene Turner (OARS, Cambridge, Massachusetts, 1986); also published in *The Uncertain Certainty* (see under Primary Works/Prose/Books/In English).

'Reading Philosophy at Night', *The Best American Essays, 1988*, edited by Annie Dillard (Ticknor & Fields, New York, 1988): 307-314; also published in *Antaeus* (see under Primary Works/Magazine Articles, Review, etc); also published in *Wonderful Words, Silent Truth* (see under Primary Works/Prose/Books/In English).

'Shop, le Bacarès, Pyrénées-Orientales, France, 1950', *Paul Strand: Essays on His Life and Work*, edited by Maren Stange (Aperture, New York, 1990).

Pesma o Kosovu: Savremena Srpska Poezija / The Poem of Kosovo, Contemporary Serbian Poetry, edited by Slobodan Vuksanovic, translated by Irena Kostic (Vidici Srpska Knjizevna Zadruga, Beograd, 1991).

'At the Bomb Testing Site', *On William Stafford: The Worth of Things*, edited by Tom Andrews (University of Michigan Press, Ann Arbor, 1993); also published in *Field: Contemporary Poetry and Poetics* (see under Primary Works/Magazine Articles, Reviews, etc); also published in *Wonderful Words, Silent Truth* (see under Primary Works/Prose/Books/In English).

'The Little Venus of the Eskimos', *The Return of the Cadavre Exquis*, edited by Jane Philbrick (Drawing Center, New York, 1993) [exhibition catalogue from the Drawing Center, New York, November 6 - December 18, 1993].

'Charles the Obscure', *The Pushcart Prize, XX*, edited by Bill Henderson (Pushcart Press, Wainscott, New York, 1995); also published in *New Letters* (see under Primary Works/Magazine Articles, Reviews, etc); also published in *Charles Simic: Essays on the Poetry*, edited by Bruce Weigl (see under Secondary Works /Books); also published in *Orphan Factory* (see under Primary Works/Prose/Books/In English).

'The Necessity of Poetry', *The Best American Essays, 1995*, edited by Jamaica Kincaid and Robert Atwan (Houghton Mifflin, Boston, 1995); also published in *Creative Nonfiction* (see under Primary Works/ Magazine Articles, Reviews, etc).

The Poet's Notebook: Excerpts from the Notebooks of 26 American Poets, edited by Stephen Kuusisto, Deborah Tall, David Weiss (W.W. Norton, New York and London, 1995): 269-290; also published as 'Poets' Notebooks' in *Orphan Factory* (see under Primary Works/Prose/Books/In English).

Ecstatic Occasions, Expedient Forms: 85 Leading Contemporary Poets Select and Comment on Their Poems, edited by David Lehman (University of Michigan Press, Ann Arbor, 1996): 183-186 [Simic discusses 'Theseus and Ariadne' and 'The Anniversary'].

'Three Fragments', *Short: A Collection of Brief Creative Nonfiction*, edited by Judith Kitchen and Mary Paumier Jones (W. W. Norton & Company, New York, 1996): 191-192 [excerpt from *The Unemployed Fortune Teller* (see under Primary Works/Prose/Books/In English).

'Dinner at Uncle Boris's', *The Best American Essays, 1997*, edited by Ian Frazier (Houghton Mifflin, Boston, 1997); also published in *Orphan Factory* (see under Primary Works/Prose/Books/In English); also published as 'Dinner at Uncle Boris'' in *Creative Nonfiction* (see under Primary Works/Magazine Articles, Reviews, etc).

'Abelardo's Poetry of Appearance', *Abelardo Morell, Face to Face: Photographs at the Gardner Museum*, Charles Simic, Jennifer R. Gross, introduction by Jill S. Medvedow (Isabella Stewart Gardner Museum,

Boston, Massachusetts, 1998).

'Refugees', *Letters of Transit: Reflections on Exile and Memory*, edited by André Aciman (New Press, New York, 1999/I.B. Tauris, London, 1999).

'Verbal Image', *Reflections in a Glass Eye: Works from the International Center of Photography Collection*, edited by Ellen Handy (Bulfinch Press, Boston, Massachusetts, 1999).

'Cops', *Writers at the Movies: Twenty-Six Contemporary Authors Celebrate Twenty-Six Memorable Movies*, edited by Jim Shepard (Perennial, New York, 2000): 242-248.

'The Soul Stays at Home', *Jane Freilicher: New Work*, (Tibor de Nagy Gallery, New York, 2000) [published in association with the exhibition *Jane Freilicher: New Work*, 16 March-22 April 2000].

'Welcome Back Mr Devi – on Alfred Brendel' [one of two essays (the other by Yves Bonnefoy) in an exhibition catalogue for *Von Teufeln Devils' Pageant*, a collaborative exhibition involving the artist George Nama and the pianist and poet Alfred Brendel held at the Jack Rutberg Fine Arts Gallery in Los Angeles between 6 April and 31 May 2002].

Prefaces, Introductions, Forewords

'Introduction', *Homage to the Lame Wolf: Selected Poems, 1956-1975*, by Vasko Popa, translated by Simic, [Field Translation Series, 2] (Oberlin College, Oberlin, Ohio, 1979).

'Introduction', *From the Hidden Storehouse: Selected Poems by Benjamin Péret*, translated by Keith Hollaman, [Field Translation Series, 6] (Oberlin College, Oberlin, Ohio, 1981).

'Introduction', *Roll Call of Mirrors: Selected Poems of Ivan V. Lalic*, translated by Charles Simic, (Wesleyan University Press, Middletown, Connecticut, 1988); also published in *Wonderful Words, Silent Truth* (see under Primary Works/Prose/Books/In English).

'Serbian Heroic Ballads', preface to *The Battle of Kosovo* (Swallow Press/Ohio University Press, Athens, 1988): 108-112; also published in *Wonderful Words, Silent Truth* (see under Primary Works/Prose/Books/In English).

'Thomas Campion', introduction to *The Essential Campion*, selected and introduced by Simic, 1988 (see under Primary Works/Prose/Books Edited or Selected by Simic).

'Foreword', *Some Other Wine and Light*, by Aleksandar Ristovic, translated by Simic (Charioteer Press, Washington D.C., 1989); also published in *Wonderful Words, Silent Truth* (see under Primary Works/Prose/Books/In English).

'Introduction', *Bright Moves*, by J. Allyn Rosser (Northeastern University Press, Boston, Massuchusetts, 1990) (see also under Primary Works/Poetry/Editions and Selections by Simic/In English).

'Introduction', *Homage to a Cat: As It Were: Logscapes of the Lost Ages*, by Vernon Newton, (Northern Lights, Orono, Maine, 1991) [limited to 1,000 hand-numbered copies].

'Introduction', *Night Mail*, by Novica Tadic, translated by Simic, [Field Translation Series, 19] (Oberlin College Press, Oberlin, Ohio, 1992).

'Introduction', *Red Knight: Serbian Women's Songs*, by Vuk Stefanovic Karadzic, edited and translated by Daniel Weissbort and Tomislav Longinovic (Menard Press, London, 1992).

'Introduction', *Sigmund Abeles*, by Robert M. Doty (New England College Gallery, Henniker, New York, 1992).

'Preface', *The Quest for Roots: The Poetry of Vasko Popa*, by Anita Lekic (Peter Lang, New York, 1993).

'Preface', *Anxious Moments*, by Ales Debeljak, translated by Christopher Merrill (White Pine Press, Fredonia, New York, 1994).

'Preface', *Prisoners of Freedom: Contemporary Slovenian Poetry*, edited by Ales Debeljak (Pedernal, Santa Fe, New Mexico, 1994).

'Foreword', *Songs in Flight: The Collected Poems of Ingeborg Bachmann*, by Ingeborg Bachmann, translated and introduced by Peter Filkins (Marsilio Publishers, New York, 1994); also published in *Orphan Factory* (see under Primary Works/Prose/Books/In English).

'Preface', *The Poet's Notebook: Excerpts from the Notebooks of 26 American Poets*, edited by Stephen Kuusisto, Deborah Tall, David Weiss (W.W. Norton, New York and London, 1995): ix-xi.

'Foreword', *Words Are Something Else*, by David Albahari, translated by Ellen Elias-Bursac, edited by Tomislav Longinovic (Northwestern University Press, Evanston, Illinois, 1996).

'A Long Course in Miracles', introduction to *Pretty Happy!*, Peter Johnson (White Pine Press, Fredonia, 1997): 15-17.

'Foreword', *The Hour Between Dog and Wolf: Poems*, by Laure-Anne Bosselaar (BOA Editions, Rochester,

New York, 1997).

'Foreword', *The Prince of Fire: An Anthology of Contemporary Serbian Short Stories*, edited by Radmila J. Gorup and Nadezda Obradovic (University of Pittsburgh Press, Pittsburgh, 1998): ix-xi.

Reid, Christopher, *Mermaids Explained* (Harcourt, New York, 2001).

MAGAZINE ARTICLES, REVIEWS, ETC

AKZENTE

'Der Minotaurus liebt sein Labyrinth'. 48:1, 2001: 57-70; also published as 'The Minotaur Loves His Labyrinth' in *The Unemployed Fortune Teller* (see under Primary Works/Prose/Books).

ARTFORUM INTERNATIONAL

'Eva Hesse', 37:10, Summer 1999: 136-137.

'When Words Don't Fail: *Artforum* Contributors Read 9-11-01', 40:3, November 2001: 33, 35-36, 39, 41-42, 46, 172-173 [Simic is one of several authors contributing to this article. His work can be found on p. 33].

ANTAEUS

'Reading Philosophy at Night', 1987; also published in *The Best American Essays, 1988*, edited by Annie Dillard (see under Primary Works/Books and Catalogues Contributed To); also published in *Wonderful Words, Silent Truth* (see under Primary Works/Prose/Books/In English).

'Negative Capability and Its Children', 30/31, Spring 1978: 348-354; also published in *Claims for Poetry*, edited by Donald Hall (University of Michigan Press, Ann Arbor, 1982): 399-406; also published in *Tendril Magazine* (see below); also published in *Written in Water, Written in Stone*, edited by Martin Lammon (University of Michigan Press, Ann Arbor, 1996): 202-208.

'On Food and Happiness', 68, Spring 1992: 19-24.

'No Cure for the Blues', 71/72, Autumn 1993: 133-139.

'Don't Squeeze the Tomatoes!', 73/74, Spring 1994: 143-149.

BOSTON REVIEW

'Our Scandal', 22:3-4, Summer 1997: 32 [lengthy statement on the Araki Yasusada Affair].

BOULEVARD

'The Flute Player in the Pit', 7:2/3, Fall 1992: 93-97 [excerpt from the introduction to *The Best American Poetry 1992* (see under Primary Works/Books and Catalogues Contributed To)].

CHRONICLE OF HIGHER EDUCATION

'The Bombardier and His Target: 2 Poets and a Powerful Coincidence', 47:10, 3 November 2000: B12-B13 [excerpt from *A Fly in the Soup* (see under Primary Works/Prose/Books/In English); also features a piece by Richard Hugo].

COLUMBIA: A JOURNAL OF LITERATURE AND ART

'Jane Kenyon', 26, 1996: 172-173; also published in *Orphan Factory* (see under Primary Works/Prose/Books/In English).

CREATIVE NONFICTION

'The Necessity of Poetry', 2, 1995: 82-93; also published in *The Best American Essays, 1995*, edited by Jamaica Kincaid and Robert Atwan (see under Primary Works/Books and Magazines Contributed To).
'Dinner at Uncle Boris'', 7, 1997; also published as 'Dinner at Uncle Boris's' in *The Best American Essays, 1997*, edited by Ian Frazier (see under Primary Works/Books and Magazines Contributed To); also published in *Orphan Factory* (see under Primary Works/Prose/Books/In English).

DENVER QUARTERLY

'Visionaries and Anti-Visionaries', 24:1, Summer 1989: 114-123; also published in *Wonderful Words, Silent Truth* (see under Primary Works/Prose/Books/In English).
'Jimmie Rodger's Last Blue Yodel', 33:3, Fall 1998: 115-117.

FIELD: CONTEMPORARY POETRY AND POETICS

'Vasko Popa', 3, Fall 1970: 24.
'Some Thoughts About the Line', 11, Fall 1974: 62-63; also published in *A Field Guide to Contemporary Poetry and Poetics*, edited by Stuart Friebert and David Young (Longman, New York, 1980); also published in *A Field Guide to Contemporary Poetry and Poetics*, edited by Stuart Friebert, David Walker, and David Young (Oberlin College Press, Oberlin, Ohio, 1997): 93-94; also published in *The Uncertain Certainty* (see under Primary Works/Prose/Books/In English).
'Images and "Images"', 23, Fall 1980: 24-26; also published in *A Field Guide to Contemporary Poetry and Poetics*, edited by Stuart Friebert and David Young (Longman, New York, 1980); also published in *A Field Guide to Contemporary Poetry and Poetics*, edited by Stuart Friebert, David Walker, and David Young (Oberlin College Press, Oberlin, Ohio, 1997): 95-97; also published in *The Uncertain Certainty* (see under Primary Works/Prose/Books/In English).
'Streets Strewn with Garbage', 29, Fall 1983: 39-40; also published in *The Uncertain Certainty* (see under Primary Works/Prose/Books/In English).
'At the Bomb Testing Site', 41, Fall 1989: 8-10; also published in *On William Stafford: The Worth of Things*, edited by Tom Andrews (University of Michigan Press, Ann Arbor, 1993) (see under Primary Works/Prose/Books and Catalogues Contributed To); also published in *Wonderful Words, Silent Truth* (see under Primary Works/Prose/Books/In English).
'My Insomnia and I', 50, Spring 1994: 53-54; also published in *Orphan Factory* (see under Primary Works/Prose/Books/In English).
'From My Notebooks: Assembly Required', 57, Fall 1997: 118; also published as 'Assembly Required' in *Orphan Factory* (see under Primary Works/Prose/Books/In English).

FRANKFURTER ALLGEMEINE ZEITUNG

'Lady Be Good', 4 March 1995: B2.
'Orphan Factory', 24 August 1995; also published in *Orphan Factory* (see under Primary Works/Prose/Books/In English).
'Ich spielte Krieg im Krieg in Belgrad', 29 April 1999: 41.
'Mit Gene Tierney in Paris', 22 July 1999: 51.
'Der Räuber Charuga', 26 February 2000: 2.
'Dieser Wahlkampf darf nie enden', 7 December 2000: 49 [American Presidential Election, 2000].
'Komischer König der Philosophen', 12 May 2001: 6 [on Buster Keaton].
'Er war ein Wilder und wollte seine Artgenossen studieren', 5 January 2002: 50 [James Atlas, *Bellow: A Biography*].

GEORGIA REVIEW

'In Praise of Folly', 52:4, Winter 1998: 703-709.

84

GETTYSBURG REVIEW

'Luneville Diary: December 1, 1962-March 1, 1963', 7:1, Winter 1994: 9-25
'New York Days, 1958-1964', 9:3, Summer 1996: 373-384; also published in *The 1998 Pushcart prize XXII*, edited by Bill Henderson (Pushcart Press, Wainscott, New York, 1997); also published in *The Pushcart Book of Essays: The Best Essays from a Quarter-Century of The Pushcart Prize*, edited by Anthony Brandt (Pushcart Press, Wainscott, New York, 2002); also published in *Orphan Factory* (see under Primary Works/Prose/Books/In English).

GRAND STREET

'Time Channel', 54, 1995: 34-35; also published in *Orphan Factory* (see under Primary Works/Prose/Books/In English).

HARPER'S MAGAZINE

'One Man's Eats', 285:1710, November 1992: 36 [excerpt from 'On Food and Happiness', published in *Antaeus* (see above)].
'On Not Thinking About Nature', 287:1719, August 1993: 28-29 [excerpt from 'Fried Sausage', published in *Ohio Review* (see below)].
'In Praise of Invective', 295:1767, August 1997: 24-27; also published in *Raritan* (see below); also published in *Thumbscrew* (see below); also published in *Orphan Factory* (see under Primary Works/Prose/Books/In English).
'How to Peel a Poem: Five Poets Dine Out on Verse', 299:1792, September 1999: 45-49, 52, 54-56, 58-60 [five poets discuss their favourite poem: Donald Hall, Cynthia Huntington, Heather McHugh, Paul Muldoon, and Simic].
'Readings: What Dreams May Come', 301:1806, November 2000: 15 [excerpt from *A Fly in the Soup* (see under Primary Works/Prose/Books/In English)].

HARVARD REVIEW

'On Dreams', 7, Fall 1994: 13-14; also published in *Orphan Factory* (see under Primary Works/Prose/Books/In English).
'Cut the Comedy', 11, Spring 1996; also published in *Orphan Factory* (see under Primary Works/Prose/Books/In English).

IRONWOOD

'Notes on Poetry and History', 24, Fall 1984: 21-24; also published in *The Uncertain Certainty* (see under Primary Works/Prose/Books/In English).
'Chinese Boxes and Puppet Theaters', 28, 1986: 104-105 [on Emily Dickinson]; also published in *Wonderful Words, Silent Truth* (see under Primary Works/Prose/Books/In English).

KAYAK

'On Cold Water', 13, January 1968: 62-63 [Lou Lipsitz, *Cold Water*].

LONDON REVIEW OF BOOKS

'Unfashionable Victims', 19:15, 31 July 1997: 12-13 [Tim Judah, *The Serbs: History, Myth and the Destruction of Yugoslavia*].
'Those Awful Serbs' [Letter to the Editor], 19:18, 18 September 1997: 4.
'Plato's Gulag' [Letter to the Editor], 20:13, 2 July 1998.

'A Suspect in the Eyes of Super-Patriots', 21:6, 18 March 1999: 26-27 [*Collected Poems of Vasko Popa*, translated by Anne Pennington, revised by Francis Jones].

'A State of One's Own' [Letter to the Editor], 21:19, 30 September 1999: 4.

'11 September: Some LRB Writers Reflect on the Reasons and Consequences', 23:19, 4 October 2001.

LOS ANGELES TIMES

'Season's Readings: Open Wounds', 4 December 1994: 8 [*Farewell to Bosnia*, photographs by Gilles Peress; *God Be with You: War in Croatia and Bosnia-Herzegovina*, photographs by Martin A. Sugarman]; also published in *Orphan Factory* (see under Primary Works/Prose/Books/In English).

MICHIGAN QUARTERLY REVIEW

'The Trouble with Poetry', 36:1, Winter 1997: 39-42; also published in *Orphan Factory* (see under Primary Works/Prose/Books/In English).

MISSOURI REVIEW

'Art Hordes', 10:3, 1987; also published in *Wonderful Words, Silent Truth* (see under Primary Works/Prose/Books/In English).

NATION

'1998 Lenore Marshall Poetry Prize', 267:14, 2 November 1998: 29 [prize awarded to *Questions for Ecclesiastes* by Mark Jarman].

NEW LETTERS

'Charles the Obscure', 60:4, Summer 1994: 21-27; also published in *The Pushcart Prize, XX*, edited by Bill Henderson (Pushcart Press, Wainscott, New York, 1995); also published in *Charles Simic: Essays on the Poetry*, edited by Bruce Weigl (see under Secondary Works/Books); also published in *Orphan Factory* (see under Primary Works/Prose/Books/In English).

NEW LITERARY HISTORY

'Composition', 9:1, Autumn 1977: 149-151; also published in *The Uncertain Certainty* (see under Primary Works/Prose/Books/In English).

'Notes on Poetry and Philosophy', 21:1, Autumn 1989: 215-221; also published in *Wonderful Words, Silent Truth* (see under Primary Works/Prose/Books/In English).

NEW REPUBLIC

'The Spider's Web', 209, 25 October 1993: 18-19.

NEW YORK REVIEW OF BOOKS

'Who Cares?', 46:16, 21 October 1999: 16 [commentary on Serbia].

'Anatomy of a Murderer', 47:1, 20 January 2000: 26-29 [Dusko Doder and Louise Branson, *Milosevic*:

Portrait of a Tyrant].

'Forgotten Games', 47:7, 27 April 2000: 4, 6-7 [Jodi Hauptman, *Joseph Cornell: Stargazing in the Cinema*].

'On the Night Train', 47:13, 10 August 2000: 52-54 [Mark Strand, *Blizzard of One: Poems*; *The Weather of Words: Poetic Invention*; *Chicken, Shadow, Moon & More*].

'Working for the Dictionary', 47:16, 19 October 2000: 9-12 [Joseph Brodsky, *Collected Poems in English, 1972-1999*, edited by Ann Kjellberg].

'Tragi-Comic Soup', 47:19, 30 November 2000: 8-11 [John Ashberry, *Other Traditions*; *Your Name Here*].

'Intensive Care', 48:3, 22 February 2001: 34-36 [Alan P. Lightman, *The Diagnosis*; *Einstein's Dreams*; *Good Benito*; *Dance for Two*].

'Miraculous Mandarin', 48:6, 12 April 2001: 6-10 [Alison Lurie, *Familiar Spirits: A Memoir of James Merrill and David Jackson*; James Merrill, *Collected Poems*, edited by J. D. McClatchy and Stephen Yenser].

'The Thinking Man's Comedy', 48:9, 31 May 2001: 13-15 [James Atlas, *Bellow: A Biography*].

'That Elusive Something', 48:12, 19 July 2001: 34-36 [James Fenton, *The Strength of Poetry*].

'Paradise Lost', 48:14, 20 September 2001: 62-64 [Roberto Calasso, *Literature and the Gods*, translated by Tim Parks].

'A World Gone Up in Smoke', 48:20, 20 December 2001: 14-18 [Czeslaw Milosz, *New and Collected Poems: 1931-2001* and *To Begin Where I Am: The Selected Essays*, edited by Bogdana Carpenter and Madeline G. Levine].

'I Know Where I'm Going', 49:3, 28 February 2002: 27-29 [James Tate, *Memoir of the Hawk: Poems*; Billy Collins, *Sailing Alone Around the Room: New and Selected Poems*].

'Divine, Superfluous Beauty', 49:6, 11 April 2002: 48 [*The Selected Poetry of Robinson Jeffers* and *The Collected Poetry of Robinson Jeffers, Volume Five: Textual Evidence and Commentary*, edited by Tim Hunt].

'The Mystery of Presence', 49:8, 9 May 2002: 24 [Adam Zagajewski, *Without End: New and Selected Poems*, translated by Clare Cavanagh, Renata Gorczynski, Benjamin Ivry, and C. K. Williams; Adam Zagajewski, *Another Beauty*, translated by Clare Cavanagh].

'The Always Vanishing World', 49:12, 18 July 2002: 44-46 [W. S. Merwin, *The Pupil* and *The Mays of Ventadorn*].

'You Can't Keep a Good Sonnet Down', 49:14, 26 September 2002: 40-42 [Gerald Stern, *American Sonnets*; April Bernard, *Swan Electric*; Charles Wright, *A Short History of the Shadow*].

New York Times

'Letters: Serbs Remember Who Sided with Nazis', 16 September 1991: 18.

'Terrifying Games', 6 December 1992: 31 [excerpt from *Dime-Store Alchemy* (see under Primary Works/Prose/Books/In English)].

New York Times Book Review

'Cats Watch Over Us', 233:6, 11 November 1990: 30 [John S. Goodall, *Puss in Boots*; Charles Perrault, *Puss in Boots*, translated by Malcolm Arthur and illustrated by Fred Marcellino].

'Verse-Case Scenarios', 21 November 1999: 46 [*One Hundred Years of Poetry for Children*, edited by Michael Harrison and Christopher Stuart-Clark; *The 20th Century Children's Poetry Treasury*, selected by Jack Prelutsky and illustrated by Meilo So].

Ohio Review

'From Notebooks 1980-1984', 43, 1989: 63.

'Fried Sausage', 49, Winter 1993.

'My Unwritten Books', 56, 1997: 57; also published in *Orphan Factory* (see under Primary Works/Prose/Books/In English).

PARIS REVIEW

'The *Octava Rima* Night Music: Lord Byron's *Don Juan*', 42:154, Spring 2000: 218-221.

PEOPLE WEEKLY

'Quote', 33:25, 25 June 1990: 28 [excerpt from *The World Doesn't End* (see under Primary Works/ Poetry/Books in English)].

PLOUGHSHARES

'Why I Like Certain Poems More Than Others', 12:3, Fall 1986: 11-12 [Simic served as guest editor of this issue]; also published in *Wonderful Words, Silent Truth* (see under Primary Works/Prose/Books/In English).

POETRY EAST

'A Retired School Teacher in Galoshes', 7, 1982; also published in *The Uncertain Certainty* (see under Primary Works/Prose/Books/In English).

QUARRY WEST

'Caballero Solo', 25, 1988: 60-61 [short essay on Pablo Neruda] ; also published in *Wonderful Words, Silent Truth* (see under Primary Works/Prose/Books/In English).

RARITAN

'In Praise of Invective', 14:3, Winter 1995: 60-64; also published in *Harper's Magazine* (see above); also published in *Thumbscrew* (see below); also published in *Orphan Factory* (see under Primary Works/ Prose/Books/In English).

TENDRIL MAGAZINE

'Negative Capability and Its Children', 18, 1984: 51-58; also published in *Antaeus* (see above); also published in *Claims for Poetry*, edited by Donald Hall (University of Michigan Press, Ann Arbor, 1982): 399-406; also published in *Written in Water, Written in Stone*, edited by Martin Lammon (University of Michigan Press, Ann Arbor, 1996): 202-208.

THUMBSCREW

'In Praise of Invective', 3, Autumn/Winter 1995: 2-9; also published in *Harper's Magazine* (see above); also published in *Raritan* (see above); also published in *Orphan Factory* (see under Primary Works/ Prose/Books/In English).
'The Mystery of Happiness', 18, Spring 2001: 17-21.

TIMES LITERARY SUPPLEMENT

'A Masquerade All Around', 5185, 16 August 2002: 23 [Saul Steinberg with Aldo Buzzi, *Reflections and Shadows*].

TIN HOUSE

'The Devil Is a Poet', 1:3, Winter 2000.
'Poetry: The Art of Memory', 2:3, Spring 2001 [on Yehuda Amichai].

VERSE

'The Poetry of Village Idiots', 13:1, 1996: 7-8; also published in *Orphan Factory* (see under Primary Works/Prose/Books/In English).

WASHINGTON POST

'Why Chicago Is ... An Immigrant's Intro to a Fearful Paradise', 18 August 1996: C1; also published as 'Fearful Paradise' in *Orphan Factory* (see under Primary Works/Prose/Books/In English).

WASHINGTON SQUARE REVIEW

'Exile: Another Incredible Country', 1:2, Spring 1965: 13.

WESTERN HUMANITIES REVIEW

'Poetry Is the Present', 45:1, Spring 1991: 16-18.

XENIA: A MAGAZINE OF POETRY AND COMMENT

'Concerning a Certain Controversy', 2, Spring 1966.

THE YALE REVIEW

'Holly Wright's Photographs of Hands', 84:4, 1996: 26-37; also published in *Orphan Factory* (see under Primary Works/Prose/Books/In English).

SOUND RECORDINGS

Charles Simic Reading His Poems with Comment (Archive of Recorded Poetry and Literature, Washington, D.C., 1973): 1 sound tape reel [Simic reads from *Dismantling the Silence*].
Poetry Reading by Charles Simic and Barbara Guest (Harvard University Library, Boston, Massachusetts, 1974).
Untitled (Academy of American Poets, New York, 1974): 1 sound cassette (60 min.) [recorded at The Donnell Library Center, April 9, 1974, with an introduction by Theodore Wilentz. Poems include: 'Tapestry', 'Two Riddles', 'Brooms', 'Travelling', 'Charles Simic', 'Further Adventures of Charles Simic', 'Invention of Nothing', 'Pain', 'Ballad', 'Breasts', 'The Point', 'Two Riddles: 2', 'The Partial Explanation', 'Animal Acts', 'Help Wanted', 'Eyes Fastened with Pins', 'A Landscape with Crutches', 'Nursery Rhyme', 'Solitude', 'Trees at Night', 'Harsh Climate', 'Ballad', 'Breasts', 'Euclid Avenue'].
John Ashbery and Charles Simic Reading and Discussing Their Poems (Archive of Recorded Poetry and Literature, Washington, D.C., 1975): 1 sound tape reel (ca. 86 min.) [poets introduced by Stanley Kunitz. Recorded in the Coolidge Auditorium at the Library of Congress in Washington, D.C. Sponsored by the Gertrude Clarke Whittall Poetry and Literature Fund].
A Poet Reads His Work: Charles Simic, [Stony Brook Visiting Poets Series, 2] (Educational Communications Center, State University of New York at Stony Brook, 1976): 1 audiocassette (51 min.) [also issued as

videocassette].

Poetry Reading by Charles Simic (Harvard University Library, Boston, Massachusetts, 1976).

Charles Simic and Marvin Bell (Harvard University Library, Boston, Massachusetts, 1977).

School for Dark Thoughts (Watershed Tapes, Washington, D.C., 1979): 1 cassette (45 min.).

Charles Simic Reads His Poetry and Announces the Winners of the Lois Morrel Poetry Prize (Swarthmore College, 1981): 1 cassette [recorded in Bond Hall, Swarthmore College, 26 February 1981].

Poetry Reading by Charles Simic and James Tate (Harvard University Library, Boston, Massachusetts, 1983).

New Letters on the Air (University of Missouri, Kansas City, Missouri, 1983) [tape of programme broadcast on 17 June 1983] (see also under Primary Works/Radio Appearances).

Charles Simic Reads His Own Poetry (Cornell University, New York, 1983).

New Letters on the Air (University of Missouri, Kansas City, Missouri, 1990) [tape of programme broadcast on 23 November 1990] (see also under Primary Works/Sound Recordings;see also under Secondary Works/Interviews).

Split Horizon [with Thomas Lux and James Tate] (Harvard University, Hilles Library Cinema, 1994) [recorded under the auspices of the Ellen Sitgreaves Vail Motter Fund for Radcliffe College and sponsored by the Woodberry Poetry Room. Poets introduced by Stratis Haviaras. Poems read include: 'Miracle Glass Company', 'Childhood at the Movies', 'Sinister Company', 'The Clocks of the Dead', 'The Church of Insomnia', 'Divine Collaborator', 'What I Overheard', 'An Address with Exclamation Points', 'Relaxing in the Mad House', 'The Philosopher', 'Where the Dreaming Wabash Flows', 'Reading History', 'The Big Cover-Up', 'Player', 'Via de tritone', 'Mystery Writer'].

Jane Kenyon: A Celebration of Her Life and Works (University of New Hampshire Library, Durham, New Hampshire, 26 October 1995): audiocassette [Mekeel McBride, Donald Hall, and Simic read Jane Kenyon's verse and relate special remembrances of her life; also available as videocassette].

Poetry Reading (Harvard University, Cambridge, Massachusetts, 1996): 1 sound tape reel (48 min.) [sponsored by the Yugoslav Cultural Club and recorded for the Woodberry Poetry Room at Harvard College Library on 2 May 1996 in the Lamont Library Forum Room, Harvard University. Simic reads his English translations from various anthologies of Serbian and Yugoslavian poetry, including 'Phaedrus' by Jovan Hristic; 'History' by Tomz Sacamun; 'Ante Psalm', 'Toys, Dream', and 'Text, Silk' by Novica Tadic; 'Master, Blow Out the Candle', 'A Feast Full of Expectations', and 'Out of the Microscope' by Slavko Mihalic; 'A Poem with Guilt in the Title' by Nina Zivancevic; 'The Law', 'About Debt and Other Things', 'Maids', 'Out House', 'Monastic Out House', and 'Out in the Open' by Aleksandar Ristovic. Simic also reads selections from his own poetry, including 'Prodigy', 'Baby Pictures of Famous Dictators', 'Madonnas Touched Up with a Goatee', 'Cameo Appearances', 'Late Call', 'Mirrors at 4 a.m.', 'Emily's Theme', 'Have You Met Miss Jones?', 'The Famous No Shows', and 'Little Unwritten Book'].

In Their Own Voices: A Century of Recorded Poetry, edited by Rebekah Presson (Rhino Records, Los Angeles, 1996): four cassettes/2 CDs [Simic reads 'We Were So Poor', 'I Was Stolen by the Gypsies', and 'Everybody Knows the Story'].

Donald Hall and Charles Simic Reading Their Poems in the Montpelier Room, Library of Congress, March 4, 1999 (Archive of Recorded Poetry and Literature, Washington, D.C., 1999): 1 sound tape reel (ca. 75 min.) [program introduction by Prosser Gifford; poet introductions by Robert Pinsky].

VIDEO & TELEVISION APPEARANCES

A Poet Reads His Work: Charles Simic, [Stony Brook Visiting Poets Series, 2] (Educational Communications Center, State University of New York at Stony Brook, 1976): 1 videocassette (51 min.) [also issued as audiocassette].

Seasonable Madness (Dance Theater Workshop's Economy Tires Poetry Series, New York, 1982): 1 NTSC videocassette (54 min.) [readings by John Pijewski and Simic at DTW's Bessie Schönberg Theater, New York].

Agni's Conference on Poetry and Opposition: From Romania to Roxbury, edited by Mark Wagner and Askold Melnyczuk in association with CCTV (Agni Productions, Boston, 1992).

'Culture of Violence: Conversation', McNeil/Lehrer News Hour (PBS), 29 December 1993 [Charlayne Hunter-Gault talks with Simic about his war torn birthplace, the former Yugoslavia; transcript #4825].

Jane Kenyon: A Celebration of Her Life and Works (University of New Hampshire Library, Durham, New Hampshire, 26 October 1995): videocassette [Mekeel McBride, Donald Hall, and Simic read Jane

Kenyon's verse and relate special remembrances of her life; also available as audiocassette].

The Anne Newman Sutton Weeks Poetry Series Presents Charles Simic (Westminster College of Salt Lake City, 29 November 2001): 1 videocassette (53 min.).

RADIO APPEARANCES

New Letters on the Air (Kansas City, Missouri), 17 June 1983 [Simic reads 18 of his poems; recorded at the Associated Writing Programs conference in St. Louis, Missouri] (see also under Primary Works/ Sound Recordings).

New Letters on the Air (Kansas City, Missouri, 1990), 23 November 1990 (see also under Primary Works/ Sound Recordings; see also under Secondary Works/Interviews).

Sydell, Laura, 'Poet Laureate Joseph Brodsky Dies at Age 55', *NPR: Morning Edition*, 29 January 1996 [commentary by Bob Edwards, Joseph Brodsky, Andy Carroll, and Charles Simic; transcript #1791-14].

Flatow, Ira, 'Reading of a Charles Simic Poem', *NPR: Sounds Like Science*, 3 April 1999 [reading of 'Madonnas Touched up with a Goatee' by Susan Stone].

SECONDARY WORKS

Books

Charles Simic: Essays on the Poetry, edited by Bruce Weigl (University of Michigan Press, Ann Arbor, 1996): Bruce Weigl, 'Introduction': 1-5; William Matthews, 'Charles Simic's *What the Grass Says*': 9-13; Diane Wakoski, 'Charles Simic's *Somewhere Among Us a Stone Is Taking Notes*': 14-15; Victor Contoski, 'At the Stone's Heart: Charles Simic's *Dismantling the Silence*': 16-20; Peter Schmidt, '*White*: Charles Simic's Thumbnail Epic': 21-49; George Hitchcock, 'Charles Simic's *Return to a Place Lit by a Glass of Milk*': 50-52; David Ignatow, 'Charles Simic's *Charon's Cosmology*': 53-54; Robert Shaw, 'Life among the Cockroaches: Charles Simic's *Classic Ballroom Dances* and *White (A New Version)*': 55-61; David Young, 'Charles Simic's *Classic Ballroom Dances*': 62-67; Peter Stitt, 'Imagination in the Ascendant: Charles Simic's *Austerities*': 68-69; Liam Rector, 'Charles Simic's *Selected Poems*': 70-72; Brian C. Avery, 'Unconcealed Truth: Charles Simic's *Unending Blues*': 73-95; Christopher Buckley, 'Sounds That Could Have Been Singing: Charles Simic's *The World Doesn't End*': 96-113; Thomas Lux, 'The Nature of the Pleasure: *The Book of Gods and Devils*': 114-118; Helen Vendler, 'Totemic Sifting: Charles Simic's *The Book of Gods and Devils, Hotel Insomnia,* and *Dime-Store Alchemy*': 119-132; Lisa Sack, 'Charles the Great: Charles Simic's *A Wedding in Hell*': 133-137; Robert B. Shaw, 'Charles Simic: An Appreciation': 141-147; Tomislav Longinovic, 'Between Serbian and English: The Poetics of Translation in the Works of Charles Simic': 148-155; Bruce Bond, 'Immanent Distance: Silence and the Poetry of Charles Simic': 156-163; Matthew Flamm, 'Impersonal Best: Charles Simic Loses Himself': 164-171; Jay Barwell, 'Charles Simic: Visions of Solitude': 172-182; Bruce Weigl, 'The Metaphysician in the Dark: An Interview': 208-225; Brian C. Avery, 'A Simic Bibliography': 226-233 [the book also contains three pieces by Simic: 'From Notebooks, 1963-1969': 185-192; 'From Notebooks, 1980-1984': 193-201; 'Charles the Obscure': 202-207].

SPECIAL ISSUES OF JOURNALS

Manassas Review: Essays on Contemporary American Poetry, 1:2, Winter 1978.
Harvard Review, 13, Fall 1997, *Charles Simic at Large*, edited by Stratis Haviaras.

INTERVIEWS

'An Interview with Charles Simic', *Crazy Horse*, 11, Summer 1972: 23-26; also published in *The Uncer-*

tain Certainty (see under Primary Works/Prose/Books/In English).

'Interview – Charles Simic', Sky Writing, 1:2, 1972.

Dodd, Wayne and Stanley Plumly, 'Where the Levels Meet: An Interview with Charles Simic', Ohio Review, 14:2, Winter 1973: 49-58; also published in American Poetry Observed: Poets on Their Work, edited by Joe David Bellamy (University of Illinois Press, Urbana and Chicago, 1984); also published in The Uncertain Certainty (see under Primary Works/Prose/Books/In English).

Starbuck, George, 'A Conversation', Ploughshares, 2:3, 1975: 78-91; also published in The Uncertain Certainty (see under Primary Works/Prose/Books/In English).

Steier, Rod, '"Moments Worth Preserving and Playing Again": An Interview with Charles Simic', Manassas Review: Essays on Contemporary American Poetry, 1:2, Winter 1978: 11-15; also published in The Uncertain Certainty (see under Primary Works/Prose/Books/In English).

Jackson, Rick and Michael Panori, 'The Domain of the Marvelous Prey', Poetry Miscellany, 8, 1978; also published in The Uncertain Certainty (see under Primary Works/Prose/Books/In English); also published in Acts of Mind: Conversations with Contemporary Poets (University of Alabama Press, 1983).

'An Interview with Charles Simic', Interlochen Review, 1:2, 1980; also published in The Uncertain Certainty (see under Primary Works/Prose/Books/In English).

Santos, Sherod, 'An Interview with Charles Simic', Missouri Review, 7:3, 1984: 61-74; also published in The Uncertain Certainty (see under Primary Works/Prose/Books/In English).

Zivancevic, Nina, 'Between the Languages: An Interview with Charles Simic', Poetry Flash, October 1987: I.

McQuade, Molly, 'PW Interviews: Charles Simic', Publishers Weekly, 237:44, 2 November 1990: 56-57.

Rothstein, Mervyn, 'Seeing New York with a Poet's Eye', New York Times, 9 November 1990: C1.

New Letters on the Air (Kansas City, Missouri, 1990), 23 November 1990 (see also under Primary Works/ Sound Recordings; see also under Primary Works/Radio Appearances).

Liebs, Andrew, 'An Interview with Charles Simic', The Single Hound: The Poetry & Image of Emily Dickinson, 2:2, December 1990: 8-9.

Weigl, Bruce, 'The Metaphysician in the Dark: An Interview with Charles Simic', American Poetry Review, 20:5, September—October 1991: 5-13; also published in Charles Simic: Essays on the Poetry, edited by Bruce Weigl (see under Secondary Works/Books).

'Say No to the Predictable', Sycamore Review, 4:2, Summer 1992; also published in Charles Simic: Essays on the Poetry, edited by Bruce Weigl (see under Secondary Works/Books); also published in Delicious Imaginations: Conversations with Contemporary Writers, edited by Sarah Griffiths and Kevin J. Kehrwald (NotaBell Books, West Lafayette, Indiana, 1998).

'A Conversation', Another Chicago Magazine, 26, Fall 1993: 187-195.

Williams, Eric and J. Patrick Craig, 'A Conversation with Charles Simic', Artful Dodge, 24/25, 1993: 17-28 [interview conducted on 16 March 1993 at Memphis State University as part of the River City Writer's Series. Also available online: http://www.wooster.edu/ArtfulDodge/simic.html].

Anonymous, 'Pulitzer Prize Poet Talks with GS Writers', Columbia University Record, 20:17, 17 February 1995.

Encke, Jeffrey, Ai-Jen Poo, Mary Ellen Ugactz and Joshua Green, The Observer (Columbia University), March 1995 [this consists of extracts from the full interview that was published in Quarto in the Fall of 1995; see next entry for details].

Encke, Jeffrey, Ai-Jen Poo, Mary Ellen Ugactz and Joshua Green, Quarto (Columbia University), Fall 1995.

Patterson, Nicholas, 'An Interview with Charles Simic', Chicago Literary Review, Fall 1995.

Limehouse, Capers and Megan Sexton, 'Visionary Sceptic: An Interview with Charles Simic', Atlanta Review, 2:1, 1995: 23-36.

Simic, Charles, 'Real America', An Unsentimental Education: Writers and Chicago, edited by Molly McQuade (University of Chicago Press, Chicago and London, 1995): 150-157; excerpted in Chicago Review, 41:2/3, 1995: 13-18.

Corbett, William, 'An Interview with Charles Simic', Poets & Writers, 24:3, 1 May 1996: 30.

Spalding, J.M., 'Interview: Charles Simic', The Cortland Review, 4, August 1998 [The Cortland Review is an on-line magazine: http://www.cortlandreview.com/issuefour/interview4.htm].

'The Interrogation of Charles Simic', The Writer's Chronicle, 32:1, 1999: 31.

Spiegel, Herbert, 'Fragebogen: Charles Simic, Schriftsteller', Frankfurter Allgemeine Zeitung, 20 April 2000: 11.

Hendrix, Keith, 'Loosening the Ropes: A Talk with Charles Simic', Arts & Letters: Journal of Contemporary Culture, 4, Fall 2000 [available online: http://al.gcsu.edu/hendrix4.htm].

McHenry, Eric, 'Seeing Things', *Atlantic Monthly [Atlantic Unbound]*, 10 January 2001.

Archibeque, Carlye, 'Charles Simic: Poet', *Independent Reviews Site*, 2:5, December 2001 [the *Independent Reviews Site* is an on-line magazine: http://www.theindependentreviewsite.org/v2_i5/].

Hulse, Michael, 'Charles Simic in Interview with Michael Hulse', *Leviathan Quarterly*, 2, December 2001: 83-87 [this is a short extract from an earlier version of the interview featured in this volume.]

Lysaker, John T., 'White Dawns, Black Noons, Twilit Days: Charles Simic's Poems Before Poetry', *TriQuarterly*, 110/111, Fall 2001: 525-580.

Corbett, William, 'Charles Simic: We'll Talk', *All Prose: Selected Essays and Reviews* (Zoland Books, Cambridge, Massachussetts, 2001).

Ratiner, Steven, 'The Toy of Language', *Giving Their Word: Conversations with Contemporary Poets*, edited by Steven Ratiner (University of Massachusetts Press, Amherst, 2002).

ARTICLES, ESSAYS, ENTRIES

'Charles Simic', *The Major Young Poets*, selected and introduced by Al Lee (World Publishing Company, New York, 1971): 83-105 [includes a brief biographical sketch, bibliography, and the following poems: 'Stone', 'Stone Inside a Stone', 'Coal', 'Ax', 'Forest', 'Thrush', 'The Wind', 'Sands', 'Knife', 'Fork', 'Spoon', 'Table', 'Meat', 'Butcher Shop', 'To All Hog-Raisers, My Ancestors', 'Bones', 'The Roach', 'My Shoes', 'Second Avenue Winter', 'Concerning My Neighbors, the Hittites', 'Hearing Steps', 'Five Naked Men Lined Up for Army Physicals', 'The Boss Hires', 'Working on the Pennsylvania Railroad in Winter', 'How to Psalmodize', 'Poem without a Title', and 'Inner Man'].

Foucherau, Serge, 'La nouvelle subjectivité', *Lettres Nouvelles Mercure de France*, December 1970-January 1971: 159-162.

Balakian, Anna, *Surrealism: The Road to the Absolute*, Revised edition (Dutton, New York, 1970): 25-26.

Katz, Bill, 'Little Presses', *Library Journal*, 97, 15 December 1972: 3993-3994.

Ha[zo], S[amuel], 'Literature: American Poetry', *Britannica Book of the Year, 1972* (Encyclopedia Britannica, 1972): 427-428.

'Simic, Charles 1938-', *Contemporary Authors*, volumes 29-32 (Gale Research, Detroit, 1972): 580.

Zweig, Paul, 'The New Surrealism', *Salmagundi*, 22/23, Spring/Summer 1973: 269-284.

Walker, David, 'Stone Soup: Contemporary Poetry and the Obsessive Image', *Field: Contemporary Poetry and Poetics*, 13, Fall 1975: 39-47.

Williamson, Alan, 'Silence, Surrealism, and Allegory', *kayak*, 40, November 1975: 57-67.

Shaw, Robert B., 'Charles Simic: An Appreciation', *New Republic*, 24 January 1976: 25-27; also published in *Charles Simic: Essays on the Poetry*, edited by Bruce Weigl (see under Secondary Works/Books).

'Simic, Charles 1938-', *Contemporary Literary Criticism*, volume 6, edited by Carolyn Riley and Phyllis Carmel Mandelson (Gale Research, Detroit, 1976): 501-502.

Pinsky, Robert, *The Situation of Poetry* (Princeton University Press, Princeton, New Jersey, 1976): Endnote 7, 178.

Walker, David, 'O What Solitude: The Recent Poetry of Charles Simic', *Ironwood 7/8*, 4:1-2, 1976: 61-67.

Contoski, Victor, 'Charles Simic: Language at the Stone's Heart', *Chicago Review*, 28:4, Spring 1977: 145-157.

Thurley, Geoffrey, 'Devices among Words: Kinnell, Bly, Simic', *The American Moment, American Poetry in the Mid-Century* (St Martin's Press, New York, 1977): 225-228.

Breslin, Paul, 'How to Read the New Contemporary Poem', *American Scholar*, 47, Summer 1978: 357-370.

Allen, Dick, 'The Poet's Descent and Crossing: Charon's Cosmology', *Manassas Review: Essays on Contemporary American Poetry*, 1:2, Winter 1978: 55-61.

Barwell, Jay, 'Charles Simic: Visions of Solitude', *Manassas Review: Essays on Contemporary American Poetry*, 1:2, Winter 1978: 33-44; also published in *Charles Simic: Essays on the Poetry*, edited by Bruce Weigl (see under Secondary Works/Books)

Bizzaro, Patrick. '"I Am Whatever Beast Inhabits Me": Introduction for Charles Simic', *Manassas Review: Essays on Contemporary American Poetry*, 1:2, Winter 1978: 7.

Robson, Deborah, 'Some Experiments in Alchemy', *Manassas Review: Essays on Contemporary American Poetry*, 1:2, Winter 1978: 25-31.

Smith, Arthur, 'Definitions', *Manassas Review: Essays on Contemporary American Poetry*, 1:2, Winter

1978: 45-47.

'Simic, Charles 1938-', *Contemporary Literary Criticism*, volume 9, edited by Dedria Bryfonski (Gale Research, Detroit, 1978): 478-482.

Goldensohn, Lorrie, 'Love's Progress: Women, Sex, and Poetry in the Seventies', *Agni* (Boston University), 10-11, 1979: 222-242.

Altieri, Charles, 'From Experience to Discourse: American Poetry and Poeticism in the Seventies', *Contemporary Literature*, 21, Spring 1980: 191-222.

Jackson, Richard, 'Charles Simic and Mark Strand: The Presence of Absence', *Contemporary Literature*, 21, Winter 1980: 136-145.

Mitgutsch, Waltraud, 'Metaphorical Gaps and Negation in the Poetry of W. S. Merwin, Mark Strand, and Charles Simic', *On Poets and Poetry: Second Series*, Salzburg Institut fur Anglistik und Amerikanistik, Universitat Salzburg, 1980: 3-30.

Jarman, Mark, 'The Raw Flesh in the Little Box: The Poetry of Charles Simic', *kayak*, 58, January 1982: 65-71.

Crenshaw, Brad, 'Charles Simic', *Critical Survey of Poetry*, English Language Series, volume 6, edited by Frank N. Magill (Salem Press, Inglewood Cliffs, New Jersey, 1982): 2590-2598.

'Simic, Charles 1938-', *Contemporary Literary Criticism*, volume 22, edited by Sharon R. Gunton and Jean C. Stine (Gale Research, Detroit, 1982): 379-383.

Christensen, Paul, 'Charles Simic', *Contemporary Poets*, edited by James Vinson and D. L. Kirkpatrick (St. Martin's Press, New York, 1985): 782-783.

Flamm, Matthew, 'Impersonal Best: Charles Simic Loses Himself', *Village Voice Literary Supplement*, December 1986: 18-19; also published in *Charles Simic: Essays on the Poetry*, edited by Bruce Weigl (see under Secondary Works/Books).

Holden, Jonathan, 'Poetry and Commitment', *Style and Authenticity in Post-Modern Poetry* (University of Missouri Press, Columbia, 1986).

Bond, Bruce, 'Immanent Distance: Silence and the Poetry of Charles Simic', *Mid-American Review*, 5:1, 1988: 89-96; also published in *Charles Simic: Essays on the Poetry*, edited by Bruce Weigl (see under Secondary Works/Books).

Jackson, Richard, 'An Anonymous Time: Charles Simic's Mythologies', *The Dismantling of Time in Contemporary Poetry* (University of Alabama Press, Tuscaloosa, 1988): 239-280.

'Simic, Charles 1938-', *Contemporary Literary Criticism*, volume 49, edited by Daniel G. Marowski and Roger Matuz (Gale Research, Detroit, 1988): 335-343.

Soderberg, Lasse, 'Charles Simic', *Lyrikvannen*, 35:1, 1988: 41.

Hart, Kevin, 'Writing Things: Literary Property in Heidegger and Simic', *New Literary History*, 21, Autumn 1989: 199-214.

[Cramer, Hilton], 'Notes and Comments: A Pulitzer for – What?', *New Criterion*, 8:10, June 1990: 1-2.

Fenza, D. W., 'News and Views: Totally Miffed about the Pulitzer', *Associated Writing Programs Chronicle*, 23:1, September 1990: 21-22.

Rothstein, Mervyn, 'Seeing New York with a Poet's Eye', *New York Times*, 9 November 1990: C1.

Dooley, David, 'Poetry Chronicle', *Hudson Review*, 44:1, Spring 1991: 155-163.

Nijmeijer, Peter, 'Charles Simic: Dichter tussen twee werelden (Charles Simic: A Poet Between Two Worlds)', *De Gids* (Amsterdam), 154:2, 1991: 155-162.

'Simic, Charles 1938-', *Contemporary Literary Criticism*, volume 68, edited by Roger Matuz (Gale Research, Detroit, 1991): 362-379.

Kirby, David, 'Charles Simic: May 9, 1938-', *Dictionary of Literary Biography: American Poets Since World War II, Second Series*, volume 105, edited by R. S. Gwynn (Gale Group, Detroit, 1991): 216-226.

Orlich, Ileana A., 'The Poet on a Roll: Charles Simic's "The Tomb of Stéphane Mallarmé"', *Centennial Review*, 26:2, Spring 1992: 413-428.

Revell, Donald, 'The Lesson', *Masterplots II: Poetry Series*, volume 3, edited by Frank N. Magill (Salem Press, Pasadena, California/Englewood Cliffs, New Jersey, 1992): 1219-1221.

Miller, Philip, 'Simic's "Cabbage"', *Explicator*, 51:4, Summer 1993: 257-258.

Longinovic, Tomislav, 'Between Serbian and English: The Poetics of Translation in the Works of Charles Simic', *Modern Poetry in Translation*, n.s. 3, 1993: 167-174; also published in *Charles Simic: Essays on the Poetry*, edited by Bruce Weigl (see under Secondary Works/Books).

Glover, Michael, 'Brute of a Poet', *The Independent* (London), 19 September 1995: 14 [review of a Simic reading at the Purcell Room, London].

Vargas, Rafael, 'La traduccion como puente: Proyectos y practicas', *Inti: Revista de Literatura Hispanica*,

42, Autumn 1995: 287-289.

Wright, Charles, 'Improvisations: Narrative of the Image (A Correspondence with Charles Simic)', *Gettysburg Review*, 8:1, Winter 1995: 9-21; also published in Charles Wright, *Quarter Notes: Improvisations and Interviews* (University of Michigan Press, Ann Arbor, 1995): 57-74.

McCoy, David, 'Charles Simic', *The Geometry of Blue: Prose and Selected Poems* (Spare Change Press, Massillon, Ohio, 1995).

Maio, Samuel Joseph, *Creating Another Self: Voice in Modern American Personal Poetry* (Jefferson University Press, Lanham, Maryland, 1995); also published as 'Creating Another Self: An Analysis of Voice in American Poetry' (see under Secondary Works/Dissertations).

Vendler, Helen, 'A World of Foreboding: Charles Simic', *Soul Says: On Recent Poetry* (Belknap Press of Harvard University Press, Cambridge, Massachusetts, 1995): 102-116.

Dobyns, Stephen, *Best Words, Best Order* (St Martin's Griffin, New York, 1996): 161, 169.

Heaney, Seamus, 'Shorts for Simic', *Agni* (Boston University), 44, 1996: 202-208; also published in *Harvard Review*, 13, Fall 1997: 14-20.

Kunisch, Hans-Peter, 'Streifzuge eines Einzelgängers. Zwischen Belgrad und Chicago: Lyriker Charles Simic liest in München', *Süddeutsche Zeitung*, 18 March 1996.

Morris, Daniel, '"My Shoes": Charles Simic's Self-Portraits', *A/B: Auto/Biography Studies*, 11:1, Spring 1996: 109-127.

'Manche jedoch treffen uns mitten ins Herz. Was schenkt uns die Literatur? Elf Sätze, die vom Lesen übrigbleiben Charles Simic', *Frankfurter Allgemeine Zeitung*, 24 December 1996: 26.

McNair, Wesley, 'Taking the World for Granite: Four Poets in New Hampshire', *Sewanee Review*, 104:1, Winter 1996: 70-81 [Simic is one of several New Hampshire poets discussed].

Stitt, Peter, 'Simic, Charles (1938-)', *The Oxford Companion to 20th-Century Poetry*, edited by Ian Hamilton (Oxford University Press, Oxford and New York, 1996): 490-491.

Weigl, Bruce, 'Borderline', *American Poetry Review*, 25:1, January 1996: 13-14 [excerpt from *Charles Simic: Essays on the Poetry*, edited by Bruce Weigl (see under Secondary Works/Books).]

Ingendaay, Paul, 'Katze am Schachbrett', Frankfurter Allgemeine Zeitung, 15 February 1997: B5.

Oesterle, Kurt, 'Armes Kind, das Dichter wird: Erinnerungen des amerikanischen Lyrikers Charles Simic', *Süddeutsche Zeitung*, 22 February 1997.

Hoover, Bob, 'American Surrealist: Famed Translator, Prolific Writer Charles Simic to Read at CMU', *Pittsburgh Post-Gazette*, 2 May 1997: 18.

Barr, Tina, 'The Poet As Trickster Figure, Charles Simic's Pack of Cards', *Harvard Review*, 13, Fall 1997: 84-93.

'Wunderkiste Welt. Szenen einer Kindheit: Charles Simic erinnert sich', *Neue Zürcher Zeitung*, 15 March 1997: 67.

Stitt, Peter, 'Charles Simic: Poetry in a Time of Madness', *Uncertainty & Plenitude Five Contemporary Poets* (University of Iowa Press, Iowa City, 1997): 86-118 [notes for the chapter can be found on pages 188-190].

Ingendaay, Paul, 'Die eifersüchtige Ewigkeit', *Frankfurter Allgemeine Zeitung*, 9 May 1998: 35.

Padel, Ruth, 'The Sunday Poem – No. 27: Charles Simic', *The Independent* (London), 13 June 1999: 13.

McQuade, Molly, 'The Subject of a Poem Is Astonishment: Charles Simic', *Stealing Glimpses: of Poetry, Poets, and Things in Between* (Sarabande Books, Louisville, Kentucky, 1999): 103-110.

Baker, David, *Heresy and the Ideal: On Contemporary Poetry* (University of Arkansas Press, Fayetteville, Arkansas, 2000).

Spiegel, Herbert, 'Fragebogen: Charles Simic, Schriftsteller', *Frankfurter Allgemeine Zeitung*, 20 April 2000: 11.

Mallon, Thomas, 'On Not Being a Poet', *American Scholar*, 69:2, Spring 2000: 5-11 [discusses a variety of poems by several poets, including the poetry style of Simic].

Kunisch, Hans-Peter, 'Die Geschichte probiert ihre Schere aus', *Süddeutsche Zeitung*, 30 December 2000.

Charon, Rita, 'The Seasons of the Patient-Physician Relationship', *Clinics in Heriatric Medicine*, 16:1, 2000: 37-50 [uses poems written by Simic, Wallace Stevens, and T. S. Eliot to reflect on the passage of time and human understanding].

Lucarda, Mario, 'La poesia de Charles Simic: Un acercamiento al mundo cotidiano y misterioso de uno de los esenciales poetas contemporaneos de lengua inglesa', *Quimera*, 193, 2000: 16.

Volkman, Karen, 'Charles Simic', *World Poets*, volume 3, edited by Ron Padgett (Charles Scribner's Sons, New York, 2000): 11-21.

Buruma, Ian, 'The Romance of Exile', *New Republic*, 224:7, 12 February 2001: 33-38 [discusses the nature of exile, mentioning Charles Simic and *Letters of Transit: Reflections on Exile, Identity, Language and Loss*].

'Simic, Charles 1938-', *Contemporary Authors*, New Revision Series, volume 96 (Gale Research, Detroit, 2001): 374-378.

Paloff, Benjamin, 'Charles Simic 1938-', *Encyclopaedia of American Poetry*, edited by Eric L. Haralson (Fitzroy Dearborn, Chicago/London, 2001: 665-667.

Simon, John, *Dreamers of Dreams: Essays on Poets and Poetry* (Ivan R. Dee, Chicago, 2001): 215-220 [discusses Simic's translations of some poems by Vasko Popa].

Stocks, Anthony G. and Martha Sutro, 'Simic, Charles', *Contemporary Poets*, 7th edition, edited by Thomas Riggs (St. James Press, Detroit, 2001): 1092-1095.

Van Dyke, Michael, 'A Defense of Poetry: The Prose of Charles Simic', *No Exit*, Spring 2001.

BROADSIDES FOR SIMIC

Strand, Mark, *Always: For Charles Simic* (Palaemon Press, Winston-Salem, North Carolina, 1983).

Brock, Randall, *To Charles Simic* (Toronto, 1988): 1 sheet (11 x 14 cm).

MUSICAL SETTINGS

Vosk, Jay, *A Chain of Solitary Images: For Soprano, Flute, and Contrabass* (1987) [words by Simic].

Vores, Andy, *The Little Box* (Boston, 1987) [words by Vasko Popa, translated by Simic; premiered at Boston University Concert Hall, Massachusettes, March 1988].

Vores, Andy, *Return to a Place: For Low Voice and Piano* (1988) [songs with piano, including 'Return to a Place Lit by a Glass of Milk'].

Vores, Andy, *Five Little Fly Stories* (Titchfield, 1989) [contains 'The Story' by Simic; premiered by ALEA III at the Tsai Performance Center, Boston, 10 April 1992].

Glaser, David, *Closely by the Sky: For Soprano and Violoncello* (Association for the Promotion of New Music, New York, 1996).

REVIEWS

WHAT THE GRASS SAYS (1967)

Contoski, Victor, *New American and Canadian Poetry*, 5, December 1967: 41-43.

May, Boyer James, 'Towards Print: Selected Poetries: Immediate Ancestries', *Trace*, 66, 1967-1968: 313-314.

Murray, Michele, 'Two Cheers for the Little Ones', *National Catholic Reporter*, 5 June 1968: 9.

Loonie, Janice Hays, *Opinion*, August 1968: 10.

Benedikt, Michael, 'Critic of the Month', *Poetry*, 113, December 1968: 188-215.

Matthews, William, *Lillabulero*, 2:1, Winter 1968: 41-43; also published as 'Charles Simic's *What the Grass Says*' in *Charles Simic: Essays on the Poetry*, edited by Bruce Weigl (see under Secondary Works/Books).

Robinson, Edgar, 'Nine Kayak Books', *Chicago Review*, 20:1, 1968: 116-26.

Ackerson, Duane, *Dragonfly*, 2, Summer 1969: 30-32.

Taylor, William E., 'Simic, Snodgrass, etc', *South*, 1:1, 1969: 46-50.

Blazek, Doug, 'Anti Matter! Small Presses', *Nola Express*, 6-19 February 1970: 3.

SOMEWHERE AMONG US A STONE IS TAKING NOTES (1969)

Blazek, Doug, '"I Was Out after That Speck Which Imbeds Itself in Each Moment We Live"', *Book Review*, 13, August 1970: 7.

Weeks, Ramona, 'A Gathering of Poets', *Western Humanities Review*, 24, Summer 1970: 295-301.

Ackerson, Duane, 'Kayak Press and Charles Simic', *California English Journal*, 6, October 1970: 32-36.

Wakoski, Diane, 'Songs and Notes', *Poetry*, 118:6, September 1971: 355-358; also published in *Charles Simic: Essays on the Poetry*, edited by Bruce Weigl (see under Secondary Works/Books).

Contoski, Victor, 'Somewhere among Us a Stone Is Taking Notes', *New American and Canadian Poetry*, 15, December 1971: 23-36.

Hildebrand, Tim, 'Somewhere among Us a Stone Is Taking Notes', *Mandala*, 6, 1971: 55-56.

Ransmeier, J. C., *Human Voice*, 7:2, 1971: 110-111.

DISMANTLING THE SILENCE (1971)

Anonymous, *Kirkus Review*, 38, 15 November 1970: 1283.

Anonymous, *Publisher's Weekly*, 14 December 1970: 34.

Anonymous, *Kirkus Review*, 39, 1 January 1971: 13.

Czubakowski, Janusz, 'Dismantling the Silence', *Women's Wear Daily*, 26 January 1971: 12.

Morton, Kathryn, 'A Spate of Poets New and Old', *Virginian Pilot*, 28 March 1971: 71.

Charles, John W., *Library Journal*, 95, 1 April 1971: 1273.

Vendler, Helen, 'Silence of the Spider', *Christian Science Monitor*, 15 April 1971: 63.

Anonymous, *Booklist*, 67, 1 May 1971: 724.

Naiden, James, 'Dismantling the Silence: Poet Employs Harsh Imagery', *Minneapolis Star*, 30 July 1971.

Carruth, Hayden, 'Here Today: A Poetry Chronicle', *Hudson Review*, 24, Summer 1971: 320-327.

Moramarco, Fred, 'A Gathering of Poets', *Western Humanities Review*, 25, Summer 1971: 278-83.

Oberg, Arthur, 'Strategies for Existence', *Shenandoah*, 22:4, Summer 1971: 100-107.

Raab, Lawrence, 'On the Edge of Silence', *American Scholar*, 40, Summer 1971: 538-542.

Woesner, Warren, 'Inner Passages', *Abraxas*, Summer 1971.

Rogers, Dell Marie, 'Difficult Brilliant Poetry', *News and Observer* (Raleigh, North Carolina), 5 September 1971: 8.

Johnson, Halvard, 'Living on the Home Planet', *Minnesota Review*, 1, Fall 1971: 123-128.

Hoffman, Daniel, 'To Give a Book of Poetry Is to Pay a Compliment', *Sunday Bulletin*, 5 December 1971: Section 2: 8.

Standford, Derek, *Books and Bookmen*, 17 December 1971: 70-71.

Contoski, Victor, 'At the Stone's Heart', *Modern Poetry Studies*, 2:5, 1971: 236-240; also published in *Charles Simic: Essays on the Poetry*, edited by Bruce Weigl (see under Secondary Works/Books).

Shaw, Robert B., 'The Long and Short of It', *Poetry*, 119, March 1972: 342-355.

Johnson, Joyce, 'The Flight from the Familiar: *Biography and a Lament* and *Dismantling the Silence*', *Manassas Review: Essays on Contemporary American Poetry*, 1:2, Winter 1978: 17-23 [see under Secondary Works/Articles, Essays, Entries].

WHITE (1972)

D[acey], P[hilip], 'Untitled', *Crazy Horse*, 11, Summer 1972: 27.

Guimond, James, 'Moving Heaven and Earth', *Parnassus: Poetry in Review*, 1, Fall-Winter 1972: 114-115.

Contoski, Victor, *Quixote*, 8:3, March 1974: 22-23.

Carpenter, James K., 'Charles Simic: White', *Ironwood 7/8*, 4:1-2, 1976: 72-84.

RETURN TO A PLACE LIT BY A GLASS OF MILK (1974)

Anonymous, *Kirkus Review*, 42, 1 January 1974: 46.

Stuart, Dabney, *Library Journal*, 99, 15 March 1974: 761-762.

Cole, William, 'Trade Winds', *S/R World*, 23, March 1974: 43.

Zweig, Paul, *Village Voice*, 4 April 1974: 33-34.

Offen, Ron, 'Poetry Scene', *Panorama—Chicago Daily News*, 20-21 April 1974.

Cooley, Peter, 'Self-Reflections', *North American Review*, 259:3, Fall 1974: 70-71.

Hitchcock, George, 'A Gathering of Poets', *Western Humanities Review*, 28, Autumn 1974: 403-409; also published in *Charles Simic: Essays on the Poetry*, edited by Bruce Weigl (see under Secondary Works/Books).

Atlas, James, 'Autobiography of the Present', *Poetry*, 125:5, February 1975: 295-299.

Anonymous, *Choice*, 12:1, March 1975: 78.

Anonymous, *Virginia Quarterly Review*, 51, Spring 1975: 56.

Bromwich, David, 'Book Reviews', *Georgia Review*, 30, Winter 1976: 1021.

BIOGRAPHY AND A LAMENT, POEMS 1961-1967 (1976)

Johnson, Joyce, 'The Flight from the Familiar: *Biography and a Lament* and *Dismantling the Silence*', *Manassas Review: Essays on Contemporary American Poetry*, 1:2, Winter 1978: 17-23 [see under Secondary Works/Articles, Essays, Entries].

CHARON'S COSMOLOGY (1977)

Anonymous, *Kirkus Review*, 45, 1 May 1977: 533.
Palencia, Elaine F., 'Charon's Cosmology', *Library Journal*, 102:10, 15 May 1977: 1192.
Anonymous, *Booklist*, 73, 1 June 1977: 1553.
Anonymous, *Choice*, 14, October 1977: 1055.
Wood, Susan, 'Bards of America', *Washington Post Book World*, 11 December 1977: E6.
Vendler, Helen, 'Recent Poetry: Ten Poets', *Yale Review*, 67, Autumn 1977: 72-90; also published as 'Ten Poets', *Part of Nature, Part of Us: Modern American Poets* (Harvard University Press, Cambridge, 1980): 335-72.
Ignatow, David, 'Three Poets', *New York Times Book Review*, 5 March 1978: 14; also published as 'Charles Simic's *Charon's Chronology*', *Charles Simic: Essays on the Poetry*, edited by Bruce Weigl (see under Secondary Works/Books).
Anonymous, *Nation*, 11 November 1978: 517-519.
Williamson, Alan, '"*Fool*, said my muse to me..."', *Poetry*, 133, November 1978: 100-107.
Allen, Dick, 'The Poet's Descent and Crossing: *Charon's Cosmology*', *Manassas Review: Essays on Contemporary American Poetry*, 1:2, Winter 1978: 55-61.
Gallo, Louis, 'The Cosmos According to Charon: Simic's New Book', *Manassas Review: Essays on Contemporary American Poetry*, 1:2, Winter 1978: 49-53.

CLASSIC BALLROOM DANCES (1980)

Stuttaford, Genevieve, 'Nonfiction: Classic Ballroom Dances', *Publisher's Weekly*, 218:8, 22 August 1980: 38.
Molesworth, Charles, 'Fondled Memories', *New York Times Book Review*, 12 October 1980: 16.
Hudzik, Robert, 'Book Reviews: Poetry', *Library Journal*, 105:19, 1 November 1980: 2331.
Plumly, Stanley, 'Of Lyricism, Verbal Energy, the Sonnet, and Gallows Humor', *Washington Post Book World*, 2 November 1980: 11.
Shaw, Robert B., 'Life among the Cockroaches', *New Boston Review*, March/April 1981: 27-29; also published as 'Life Among the Cockroaches: Charles Simic's *Classic Ballroom Dances* and *White (A New Version)*' in *Charles Simic: Essays on the Poetry*, edited by Bruce Weigl (see under Secondary Works/Books).
Weigl, Bruce, 'Classic Ballroom Dances', *Poet Lore*, 76:1, Spring 1981: 40.
Young, David, 'Untitled', *Field: Contemporary Poetry and Poetics*, 24, Spring 1981: 83-96; also published as 'Charles Simic's *Classic Ballroom Dances*' in *Charles Simic: Essays on the Poetry*, edited by Bruce Weigl (see under Secondary Works/Books).
Young, Vernon, 'Poetry Chronicle: The Light Is Dark Enough', *Hudson Review*, 34:1, Spring 1981: 141-154.
McClatchy, J. D., 'Figures in the Landscape', *Poetry*, 138, July 1981: 231-241.
Schiff, Jeff, 'Sleep, Simple One, Sleep', *Southwest Review*, 66, Summer 1981: 330-333.
Anonymous, *Virginia Quarterly Review*, 57, Winter 1981: 25-26.
F.W., *Mid-American Review*, 1:1, 1981: 186-188.
Balakian, Peter, 'The Trauma of Memory', *American Book Review*, 4, July 1982: 2.

WHITE: A NEW VERSION (1980)

Shaw, Robert B., 'Life among the Cockroaches', *New Boston Review*, March/April 1981: 27-29 also published as 'Life Among the Cockroaches: Charles Simic's *Classic Ballroom Dances* and *White (A New Version)*' in *Charles Simic: Essays on the Poetry*, edited by Bruce Weigl (see under Secondary

Works/Books).

Schmidt, Peter, '*White*: Charles Simic's Thumbnail Epic', *Contemporary Literature*, 23:4, Fall 1982: 528-549; also published in *Charles Simic: Essays on the Poetry*, edited by Bruce Weigl (see under Secondary Works/Books).

Muratori, Fred, *Northwest Review*, 22:3, 1984: 121-125.

AUSTERITIES (1982; 1983)

Bennett, Bruce, 'Poems Magical, Poems Mordant', *Nation*, 12 March 1983: 314-315.

Williamson, Alan, 'Pasts That Stay Present', *New York Times Book Review*, 1 May 1983: 15.

Larrissy, Edward, 'Home and Abroad', *Poetry Review*, 73:2, June 1983: 64.

Rosenberg, L. M., *Chicago Tribune Book World*, 12 June 1983: 36; syndicated as 'From 5 Poets: Delights and Disappointments', *Philadelphia Inquirer*, 27 April 1983: 7.

Hulse, Michael, 'Hearing the Tones', *The Literary Review*, 61, July 1983.

Rogers, David, *World Literature Today*, 57, Summer 1983: 461.

Stitt, Peter, 'Imagination in the Ascendant', *Poetry*, 143:1, October 1983: 39-50; also published as 'Imagination in the Ascendant: Charles Simic's *Austerities*' in *Charles Simic: Essays on the Poetry*, edited by Bruce Weigl (see under Secondary Works/Books).

Anonymous, *Virginia Quarterly Review*, 59, Winter 1983: 20.

WEATHER FORECAST FOR UTOPIA AND VICINITY, POEMS 1967-1982 (1983)

Anonymous, 'Poetry: Weather Forecast for Utopia and Vicinity: Poems 1967-1982', *Publisher's Weekly*, 224:18, 28 October 1983: 67-68.

Berman, Paul, 'Brief Encounters', *Village Voice*, 28 February 1984: 46.

Pritchard, William H., 'Aboard the Poetry Omnibus', *Hudson Review*, 37, Summer 1984: 327-342.

Economou, George, *World Literature Today*, 58, Autumn 1984: 609-610.

THE UNCERTAIN CERTAINTY: INTERVIEWS, ESSAYS, AND NOTES ON POETRY (1985)

Marsh, William, 'Charles Simic: The Uncertain Certainty', *North Dakota Quarterly*, 57:1, Winter 1989: 224.

SELECTED POEMS, 1963-1983 (1985; 1986)

Anonymous, 'Poetry: Selected Poems 1963-1983', *Publisher's Weekly*, 228:4, 26 July 1985: 160-161.

Hudzik, Robert, 'Poetry', *Library Journal*, 110:15, 15 September 1985: 84-85.

Libby, Anthony, 'Gloomy Runes and Loony Spoons', *New York Times Book Review*, 12 January 1986: 17.

Funsten, Kenneth, 'Selected Poems, 1963-1983', *Los Angeles Times Book Review*, 16 March 1986: 9.

Davison, Peter, 'Poets of Exile and Isolation', *Washington Post Book World*, 13 April 1986: 6-7.

Thomas, Harry, *Boston Review*, April 1986: 28.

Stitt, Peter, 'Staying at Home and Going Away', *Georgia Review*, 40, Summer 1986: 557-571.

Bedient, Calvin, 'Burning Alone', *Sewanee Review*, 94, Fall 1986: 657-668.

Rector, Liam, 'Poetry Chronicle', *Hudson Review*, 39, Autumn 1986: 501-515; also published as 'Charles Simic's *Selected Poems*' in *Charles Simic: Essays on the Poetry*, edited by Bruce Weigl (see under Secondary Works/Books).

Milburn, Michael, 'Fresh Forks & Original Vision', *New Letters Review of Books*, 1:1, Spring 1987: 10.

Pybus, Rodney, 'Poetry Chronicle II', *Stand*, 29:3, Summer 1988: 72-80.

Hoffert, Barbara, 'Poetry', *Library Journal*, 122:6, 1 April 1997: 95.

UNENDING BLUES (1986)

Atwan, Robert, 'Unending Blues', *Los Angeles Times Book Review*, 7 December 1986: 8.

Allen, Frank, 'Poetry', *Library Journal*, 111:20, December 1986: 116.

Stitt, Peter, 'The Whirlpool of Image and Narrative Flow', *Georgia Review*, 41:1, Spring 1987: 192-208.

Young, David, 'The Naturalizing of Surrealism', *Field: Contemporary Poetry and Poetics*, 36, Spring 1987: 90-107.

Shaw, Robert B., 'Short Reviews', *Poetry*, 150:4, July 1987: 226-241 [Simic reviewed on pp. 228-230].

Dobyns, Steven, 'Some Happy Moments, Some Very Tall Language', *New York Times Book Review*, 18 October 1987: 46.

McDuff, David, 'Poetry Chronicle I', *Stand*, 29:4, Autumn 1988: 61-69.

Older, Julia, 'High Latitudes: Recent Books from Four New England Poets', *Literary Review*, 31, 1988: 358-362.

Revell, Donald, '"The Deep En-leaving Has Now Come": Ammons, Matthews, Simic, and Cole', *Ohio Review*, 41, 1988: 116-132.

THE WORLD DOESN'T END (1989)

Kaganoff, Penny, 'Poetry: The World Doesn't End', *Publisher's Weekly*, 235:5, 3 February 1989: 101-102.

Elledge, Jim, 'The World Doesn't End', *Booklist*, 85, 1 March 1989: 1087.

Allen, Frank, 'Poetry', *Library Journal*, 114:5, 15 March 1989: 74.

Gates, D., 'Pigs' Feet and Painted Sparrows', *Newsweek*, 113:12, 20 March 1989: 80.

Ash, John, 'The Shock of the New', *Washington Post Book World*, 7 May 1989: 10.

Bruckner, D. J. R., 'The Smiles and Chills in the Poetry of Charles Simic', *New York Times*, 28 May 1990: 11.

Turner, Alberta, 'Two Selves', *Field: Contemporary Poetry and Poetics*, 42, Spring 1990: 73-81.

Dooley, David, 'Poetry Chronicle', *Hudson Review*, 44:1, Spring 1991: 155-163.

Starkey, David, 'Book Reviews – The World Doesn't End', *Southern Humanities Review*, 25:1, Winter 1991: 101-102.

Gwynn, R. S., 'No Biz Like Po' Biz', *Sewanee Review*, 100:2, Spring 1992: 311-323.

THE BOOK OF GODS AND DEVILS (1990)

Rungren, Lawrence, 'Book Reviews: Arts & Humanities', *Library Journal*, 115:14, 1 September 1990: 224.

Kaganoff, Penny, 'Forecasts: Paperbacks', *Publishers Weekly*, 237:41, 12 October 1990: 57.

Kirby, David, 'Life's Goofy Splendors', *New York Times Book Review*, 23 December 1990: 16.

Passaro, Vince, 'Romantics of the Here and Now', *Newsday*, 23 December 1990: 18.

Janas, Marci, 'The Secret World of Charles Simic', *Field: Contemporary Poetry and Poetics*, 44, Spring 1991: 67-76.

Cramer, Steven, 'Goddesses, Gods, and Devils', *Poetry*, 159:4, January 1992: 227-234.

Hart, Henry, 'Story-Tellers, Myth-Makers, Truth-Sayers', *New England Review*, 15:4, Fall 1993: 192-206.

Vendler, Helen, 'Totemic Shifting', *Parnassus: Poetry in Review*, 18:2-19:1, Fall 1993: 86-99; also published as 'Totemic Shifting: Charles Simic's *The Book of Gods and Devils*, *Hotel Insomnia*, and *Dime-Store Alchemy*' in *Charles Simic: Essays on the Poetry*, edited by Bruce Weigl (see under Secondary Works/Books).

'Immer naeher ans Wort', *Süddeutsche Zeitung*, 4 December 1993.

WONDERFUL WORDS, SILENT TRUTH: ESSAYS ON POETRY AND A MEMOIR (1990)

'A Poet on Poetry, a Lawyer on the Law', *Boston Globe*, 27 May 1990: A19.

HOTEL INSOMNIA (1992)

Stenstrom, Christine, 'Book Reviews: Arts & Humanities', *Library Journal*, 117:13, 1 August 1992: 106.

Steinberg, Sybil, 'Fiction – Hotel Insomnia', *Publishers Weekly*, 239:42, 21 September 1992: 78-79.

Seaman, Donna, 'Poetry – Hotel Insomnia', *Booklist*, 89:3, 1 October 1992: 230-231.

McQuade, Molly, 'Poetry – Hotel Insomnia', *Publishers Weekly*, 239:48, 2 November 1992: 44.

Taylor, Robert, 'Charles Simic Uses Art to Light up Night', *Boston Globe*, 23 December 1992: 39.

Krusoe, James, 'Poetry for a New Year: Wake-Up Call', *Los Angeles Times*, 27 December 1992: 1.

Ott, Bill, 'Poetry – Hotel Insomnia', *Booklist*, 89:10, 15 January 1993: 838.

Zeidner, Lisa, 'Empty Beds, Empty Nests, Empty Cities', *New York Times Book Review*, 21 March 1993: 14.

Anonymous, 'Notes on Current Books: Poetry', *Virginia Quarterly Review*, 69:2, Spring 1993: 64-65.

Anderson, Scott Edward, *Bloomsbury Review*, 13:6, November—December 1993: 12.

Vendler, Helen, 'Totemic Shifting', *Parnassus: Poetry in Review*, 18:2-19:1, 1993: 86-99; also published as 'Totemic Shifting: Charles Simic's *The Book of Gods and Devils, Hotel Insomnia*, and *Dime-Store Alchemy*' in *Charles Simic: Essays on the Poetry*, edited by Bruce Weigl (see under Secondary Works/Books).

DIME-STORE ALCHEMY: THE ART OF JOSEPH CORNELL (1992)

Stuttaford, Genevieve, 'Nonfiction – Dime-Store Alchemy: The Art of Joseph Cornell', *Publishers Weekly*, 239:49, 9 November 1992: 68.

Hirsch, Edward, 'Joseph Cornell: Naked in Arcadia', *New Yorker*, 68:44, 21 December 1992: 130-134.

Taylor, Robert, 'Charles Simic Uses Art to Light up Night', *Boston Globe*, 23 December 1992: 39.

Jones, Malcolm Jr., 'Gifts That Keep on Giving', *Newsweek*, 120:26, 28 December 1992: 60.

Danto, Arthur C., 'The Art of Giving', *Harper's Bazaar*, 125:3372, December 1992: 61-62.

Als, Hilton, 'Little Boxes – Dime-Store Alchemy: The Art of Joseph Cornell', *Village Voice*, 38:14, 6 April 1993: 63-64.

Malin, Irving, 'Book Reviews', *Review of Contemporary Fiction*, 13:2, Spring 1993: 267.

Anonymous, 'Poetry – Dime-Store Alchemy by Charles Simic', *Virginia Quarterly Review*, 69:3, Summer 1993: 99.

Henry, Brian, *Richmond Times Dispatch*, 16 September 1993.

Vendler, Helen, 'Totemic Shifting', *Parnassus: Poetry in Review*, 18:2-19-1, 1993: 86-99; also published as 'Totemic Shifting: Charles Simic's *The Book of Gods and Devils, Hotel Insomnia*, and *Dime-Store Alchemy*' in *Charles Simic: Essays on the Poetry*, edited by Bruce Weigl (see under Secondary Works/Books).

Martinez, Dionisio D., 'Books', *Art Papers*, 18, January-February 1994: 59.

Dieckmann, Katherine, 'City of Women', *Village Voice*, 39:6, 8 February 1994: 22.

Barolsky, Paul, 'Writing Art History', *Art Bulletin*, 78:3, September 1996: 398-400.

Negroni, Maria, 'Joseph Cornell y Charles Simic: El arte del ladron', *Tokonoma: Traduccion y Literatura*, 5, 1997: 94-100 [compares Simic's *Dime-Store Alchemy* with the work of Joseph Cornell; Includes an excerpt in Spanish].

Morris, Daniel, 'Responsible Viewing: Charles Simic's *Dime-Store Alchemy: The Art of Joseph Cornell*', *Papers on Language & Literature*, 34:4, Fall 1998: 337-357.

Giger, R., 'Kunst zur Sprache bringen: Charles Simics literarische Hommage an Joseph Cornell', *Neue Zürcher Zeitung*, 7 October 1999: 67.

BEST AMERICAN POETRY (1992)

Kaganoff, Penny, 'Forecasts: Paperbacks', *Publishers Weekly*, 239:32/33, 20 July 1992: 244.

Muratori, Fred, 'Book Reviews: Arts & Humanities', *Library Journal*, 117:14, 1 September 1992: 179.

Anonymous, 'Poetry — Best Poems 1992 Edited by Charles Simic', *Virginia Quarterly Review*, 69:2, Spring 1993: 63-64.

A WEDDING IN HELL (1994)

Seaman, Donna, 'Poetry – A Wedding in Hell', *Booklist*, 91:4, 15 October 1994: 396.

McQuade, Molly, 'Poetry – A Wedding in Hell', *Publishers Weekly*, 241:44, 31 October 1994: 53.

Ellis, Steven R., 'Book Reviews: Arts & Humanities', *Library Journal*, 119:18, 1 November 1994: 80.

Sack, Lisa, 'Charles the Great', *Village Voice Literary Supplement*, 39:45, November 1994: 35; also published as 'Charles the Great: Charles Simic's *A Wedding in Hell*' in *Charles Simic: Essays on the Poetry*, edited by Bruce Weigl (see under Secondary Works/Books).

Merrill, Christopher, 'Moments Frozen in Time', *Los Angeles Times Book Review*, 19 March 1995: 8.

Cayton, R. F., 'English & American – A Wedding in Hell: Poems', *Choice*, 32:8, April 1995: 1305-1306.

Anonymous, 'Poetry – *A Wedding in Hell* by Charles Simic', *Virginia Quarterly Review*, 71:2, Spring

1995: SS65.

Kitchen, Judith, 'A Terrible Beauty: The Politics in Poetry', *Georgia Review*, 49:4, Winter 1995: 938-941.

Sofield, David, 'Poetry Books', *America*, 174:1, 13-20 January 1996: 16-20.

Baker, David, 'On Restraint', *Poetry*, 168:1, April 1996: 33-47; also published in David Baker, *Heresy and the Ideal: On Contemporary Poetry* (University of Arkansas Press, Fayetteville, Arkansas, 2000) (see under Secondary Works/Articles, Essays, Entries).

Speirs, Logan, 'Current Literature 1994', *English Studies*, 77:5, September 1996: 454-483.

THE UNEMPLOYED FORTUNE-TELLER: ESSAYS AND MEMOIRS (1994)

Simson, Maria, 'Paperbacks – The Unemployed Fortune Teller: Essays and Memoirs', *Publishers Weekly*, 241:41, 10 October 1994: 68.

Gargan, William, 'Literature', *Library Journal*, 119:19, 15 November 1994: 66.

Merrill, Christopher, 'Moments Frozen in Time', *Los Angeles Times Book Review*, 19 March 1995: 8.

Henry, Brian, *Richmond Times Dispatch*, 21 May 1995.

Ford, Mark, 'The Muse As Cook', *Times Literary Supplement*, 4814, 7 July 1995: 15.

Leddy, Michael, 'English – The Unemployed Fortune-Teller: Essays and Memoirs by Charles Simic', *World Literature Today*, 69:4, Autumn 1995: 805.

FRIGHTENING TOYS (1995)

Ford, Mark, 'The Muse As Cook', *Times Literary Supplement*, 4814, 7 July 1995: 15.

Anonymous, 'American Poets: Lost Voices', *Economist*, 336:7922, 8 July 1995: 82.

O'Driscoll, Dennis, 'At the Pig and Angel', *Poetry Review*, 85:2, Summer 1995: 38-40 [also includes poems by Simic].

Sansom, Ian, 'Cheesespreadology', *London Review of Books*, 18:5, 7 March 1996: 26-27.

ON THE MUSIC OF THE SPHERES (1996)

Molnar, Michael R., 'Cosmic Duets by the Two Cultures', *Mercury*, 26:6, November—December 1997: 33.

WALKING THE BLACK CAT (1996)

Brainard, Dulcy, 'Walking the Black Cat', *Publishers Weekly*, 243:40, 30 September 1996: 82.

Seaman, Donna, 'Walking the Black Cat', *Booklist*, 93:3, 1 October 1996: 317.

Zoller, James A., 'Walking the Black Cat', *Library Journal*, 121:18, 1 November 1996: 71-72.

Brainard, Dulcy, 'Walking the Black Cat', *Publishers Weekly*, 243:45, 4 November 1996: 47.

'Walking the Black Cat', *New Yorker*, 72:39, 16 December 1996: 109.

Logan, William, 'Old Guys', *New Criterion*, 15, December 1996: 61-68 [critique of several poets, including A. R. Ammons, Robert Haas, C. K. Williams, and Charles Simic].

'Editor's Corner', *Ploughshares*, 22:4, Winter 1996-1997: 233.

Guenther, Charles, 'Poetry of Charles Simic: A Kind of Magic', *St. Louis Post-Dispatch*, 2 February 1997: 5.

Jensen, Jeff, 'Walking the Black Cat', *Magill Book Reviews*, 1 April 1997.

'Walking the Black Cat', *People Weekly*, 47:17, 5 May 1997: 40.

'Notes on Current Books: Poetry', *Virginia Quarterly Review*, 73:2, Spring 1997: 63-64.

Breslin, Paul, 'Four and a Half Books', *Poetry*, 170:4, July 1997: 226-239.

Nash, Susan Smith, 'English: Verse', *World Literature Today*, 71:4, Autumn 1997: 793-794.

Cabaneiro, Dyani, 'The Anatomy of Un-Luck', *BusinessWorld*, 24 May 2002: 30.

LOOKING FOR TROUBLE (1997)

Sandom, Ian, 'Time to Get Personal', *Guardian*, 4 December 1997: 14.

Glover, Michael, 'Poetry Books', *New Statesman*, 126:4363, 5 December 1997: 59.

O'Driscoll, Dennis, 'Pages from a Dreambook', *Times Literary Supplement*, 4950, 13 February 1998: 25.
James, Stephen, 'Poetry in Space', *Thumbscrew*, 10, Spring/Summer 1998: 82-85.
Robinson, Peter, 'What's the Big Idea?', *Cambridge Quarterly*, 28:4, December 1999: 374-382.

ORPHAN FACTORY (1998)

'Forecasts: Nonfiction', *Publishers Weekly*, 244:35, 25 August 1997: 54.
Kelly, Robert, 'Book Reviews: Arts & Humanities', *Library Journal*, 122:18, 1 November 1997: 74-75.
Henry, Brian, 'Book Reviews', *Harvard Review*, 13, Fall 1997.
Nash, Susan Smith, 'World Literature in Review: English', *World Literature Today*, 72:2, Spring 1998: 383.

JACKSTRAWS (1999)

'Poetry: Jackstraws', *Publishers Weekly*, 246:8, 22 February 1999: 87.
Muratori, Fred, 'Poetry', *Library Journal*, 124:4, 1 March 1999: 88, 90.
Seaman, Donna, 'Adult Books: New Poetry Reviews', *Booklist*, 95:14, 15 March 1999: 1279.
Miller, Pamela, 'Ondaatje, Simic Share Tough Wisdom, Spiced with Difference', *Star Tribune* (Minneapolis, MN), 11 April 1999: 16F.
Mobilio, Albert, 'Books in Brief: Fiction & Poetry', *New York Times Book Review*, 25 April 1999: 20.
Lehman, David, 'Spotlight on...Poetry', *People*, 51:15, 26 April 1999: 51.
'Jackstraws', *Kirkus Reviews*, 1 May 1999.
Vendler, Helen, '"The Voice at 3 a.m."', *New York Review of Books*, 46:10, 10 June 1999: 24-27.
Henry, Brian, *Boston Review*, 24:3-4, Summer 1999.
Clark, Tom, 'Subversive Histories', *American Poetry Review*, 28:5, September-October 1999: 7-10.
Anonymous, 'Notes on Current Books: Poetry', *Virginia Quarterly Review*, 75:4, Autumn 1999: 136-137.
Veale, Scott, 'New & Noteworthy Paperbacks', *New York Times Book Review*, 23 April 2000: 24.
'Editor's Corner', *Ploughshares*, 26:1, Spring 2000: 216.
Lawless, James, 'Simic's Words Surprise Reader from Line to Line', *The Plain Dealer*, 27 August 2000: 11.
Jackson, Richard, 'Review', *Prairie Schooner*, 74:2, Summer 2000: 190-200.
Campbell-Johnston, Rachel, 'Poetry', *The Times* (London), 16 December 2000: 18.
Nelson, Helena, 'The Jokester in the Deck', *Thumbscrew*, 18, Spring 2001: 23-27.
Brownjohn, Alan, 'Ghouls, Conundrums and Curious Bears', *Sunday Times* (London), 1 July 2001.
Thirlwell, Adam, 'Deliberate Accidents', *Times Literary Supplement*, 5127, 6 July 2001: 26.
Tromp, Ian, 'Faith in Mr Worm', *Poetry Review*, 91:3, Autumn 2001: 60-61.

A FLY IN THE SOUP (2000)

Hightower, Scott, 'A Fly in the Soup', *Library Journal*, 125:17, 15 October 2000: 71.
O'Rourke, Meghan, 'A Life Stripped Bare', *Los Angeles Times*, 1 April 2001.
Thirlwell, Adam, 'Deliberate Accidents', *Times Literary Supplement*, 5127, 6 July 2001: 26.
Hecht, Anthony, 'Treasure Box', *New York Review of Books*, 18 October 2001: 57.
Tromp, Ian, 'Faith in Mr Worm', *Poetry Review*, 91:3, Autumn 2001: 60-61.
'The Best Books of 2001: Nonfiction', *Los Angeles Times*, 2 December 2001: 17.
Cox, C. Brian, 'Victims and Survivors', *Sewanee Review*, 110:1, Winter 2002: 150-157.

SELECTED EARLY POEMS (2000)

'Charles Simic: Selected Early Poems', *Kirkus Reviews*, 1 December 1999.
'January Collections', *Publishers Weekly*, 247:2, 10 January 2000: 60.
Kirsch, Adam, 'Arriving Inside the Object', *New York Times Book Review*, 16 April 2000: 23.

NIGHT PICNIC (2001)

Scharf, Michael, 'Night Picnic', *Publishers Weekly*, 248:25, 18 June 2001: 76.

Seaman, Donna, 'Adult Books: Nonfiction', *Booklist*, 97:22, August 2001: 2078.

Muratori, Fred, 'Night Picnic', *Library Journal*, 126:14, 1 September 2001: 185.

Hecht, Anthony, 'Treasure Box', *New York Review of Books*, 18 October 2001: 57.

Macklin, Elizabeth, 'A Multitude of Sins', *New York Times Book Review*, 21 October 2001: 15.

Schrom, Benjamin, 'Simic's "Picnic Night" Provides Dark Comforts', *The Yale Herald*, 26 October 2001 [*The Yale Herald* is an on-line magazine: http://www.yaleherald.com/archive/xxxii/10.26.01/ae/ p18simic.html].

Caplan, David, 'One Sunny, One from Shadows: Volumes Span Spectrum of Style', *Columbus Dispatch*, 28 October 2001: 9.

'Best Books 2001', *St. Louis Post-Dispatch*, 25 November 2001: G10.

Guenther, Charles, 'Browsing Poetry: Imaginative New Poetry Encompass the Spectrum of Life', *St. Louis Post-Dispatch*, 30 December 2001: G10.

Handler, Daniel, 'Our Favorite Books of 2001', *Newsday*, 30 December 2001: B12.

'Editor's Corner', *Ploughshares*, 27:4, Winter 2001-2002: 202.

McQuade, Molly, 'Outside the Box', *Washington Post Book World*, 20 January 2002: T13.

Thorpe, Peter, 'Brief Reviews', *Rocky Mountain News* (Denver, Colorado), 15 February 2002: 30.

Ciuraru, Carmela, 'It's a Good Month to Break Out the Verses', *San Diego Union-Tribune*, 31 March 2002: 7.

Yenser, Stephen, 'Poetry in Review', *Yale Review*, 90:2, April 2002: 171-181.

Schuldt, M.L., 'Even Less Than Usual', *Tucson Weekly*, 4-10 April 2002.

Parini, Jay, 'A "Thirst for the Divine"', *The Nation*, 274:19, 20 May 2002: 30-32.

Doreski, William, 'Book Reviews', *Harvard Review*, Spring 2002.

DISSERTATIONS

Carpenter, James K., 'The Poetry of Charles Simic', M.A. Thesis, California State College, Sonoma, 1975.

Behm, Richard H., 'A Study of the Function of Myth in the Work of Four Contemporary Poets: Charles Simic, Galway Kinnell, Gary Snyder, and Robert Duncan', Ph.D. Dissertation, Bowling Green University, 1976.

Clark, Denise, 'Charles Simic: Trends toward an International Poetry', M.A. Thesis, Eastern Illinois University, 1982.

Jones, Jordan Douglas, 'Myth in the Poetry of Charles Simic's *Dismantling the Silence, Return to a Place Lit by a Glass of Milk,* and *White*', B.A. Thesis, California State University, Northridge, 1986.

Maio, Samuel Joseph, 'Creating Another Self: An Analysis of Voice in American Contemporary Poetry', Ph.D. Dissertation, University of Southern California, 1986 [published as *Creating Another Self: Voice in Modern American Personal Poetry* (see under Secondary Works/Articles, Essays, Entries)

Prine, Jeanne Suzanne, 'Inside and Outside: The Romantic Tradition from Wordsworth to Wright', Ph.D. Dissertation, University of Georgia, 1990.

Johnson, Kent Linwood, 'Strategies of Saying: Essays and Paraessays on Formal Semantics in Twentieth Century Poetry', Ph.D. Dissertation, Bowling Green State University, 1991.

Heilker, Paul, 'Rehabilitating the Essay: An Alternative Form for Composition Instruction', Ph.D. Dissertation, Texas Christian University, 1992.

Hufstader, Jonathan, 'Coming to Consciousness: Lyric Poetry as Social Discourse in the Work of Charles Simic, Seamus Heaney, Tom Paulin, Tony Harrison, and Rita Dove', Ph.D. Dissertation, Harvard University, 1993.

Solway, Arthur, 'The Clock Behind the Blinds: A Collection of Poems', M.F.A. Thesis, Warren Wilson College, 1995 [includes a discussion of narrative and anti-narrative strategies in three poems by Simic].

Avery, Brian Charles, 'Failing to Succeed: The Poetry of Charles Simic', Ph.D. Dissertation, Pennsylvania State University, 1996.

BIBLIOGRAPHIES

'Charles Simic: Bibliography', *Manassas Review: Essays on Contemporary American Poetry*, 1:2, Winter 1978: 63-67.

104

Seluzicki, Charles, 'Charles Simic: A Bibliographic Checklist', *American Book Collector*, n.s. 3:4, July-August 1982: 34-39.

Avery, Brian C., 'A Simic Bibliography', *Charles Simic: Essays on the Poetry*, edited by Bruce Weigl (see under Secondary Works/Books).

ARCHIVES WITH HOLDINGS OF SIMIC'S CORRESPONDENCE

Fanny Howe Papers, Department of Special Collections and University Archives, Stanford University, California: http://www.oac.cdlib.org/dynaweb/ead/stanford/mss/m0768/

William Bronk Papers, Milne Special Collections and Archives, University of New Hampshire Library: http://www.izaak.unh.edu/specoll/mancoll/bronk.htm

William Harmon Papers, Southern Historical Collection, University of North Carolina at Chapel Hill: http://www.lib.unc.edu/mss/inv/h/Harmon,William.html

THE SIMIC ARCHIVES

Charles Simic's papers are held by the Milne Special Collections and Archives in the University of New Hampshire Library: http://www.izaak.unh.edu/specoll/mancoll/poets.htm#charles

THE CRITICS

WHAT THE GRASS SAYS

"I found *What the Grass Says* exciting, even though most of the poems struck me as false. Some will complain that the style is false, but if that is true it is because, in my judgement, most of the poems are working with false content. They are exploratory poems, whose ultimate value is to find Simic's true content by following false trails to dead ends. In 'Bones' the style has the shocking inevitability of having grown out of the content. What I like in Simic's poems – even though I like few of them as objects – is his seriousness. There are no slight or occasional poems here, no chocolate-covered marshmallows. I am impatient to read more of his poems, and I hope he will give over the dreams of inert silence for poems which rise from the knowledge in that superb line in 'Bones' ('What is joy to me is grief to others')."

– William Matthews, *Lillaburlero*, 1968

SOMEWHERE AMONG US STONE IS TAKING NOTES

"I have not yet decided whether Charles Simic is America's greatest living surrealist poet, a children's writer, a religious writer, or simple-minded. My decision in this matter is irrelevant actually because, whatever he is, his poetry is cryptic and fascinating."

– Diana Wakoski, *Poetry*, 1971

DISMANTLING THE SILENCE

" ... all in all, Charles Simic writes fascinating, exciting poetry. It invests mundane objects with universal significance. One rubs them in his work and they take him above or below the earth to secret places from which he gains a new perspective. Only one or two living American poets can evoke a sense of wonder so consistently."

– Victor Contoski, *Modern Poetry Studies*, 1971

WHITE

"Helen Vendler once argued that Simic is a strong poet plagued by poems with weak endings that merely complete a 'known shape' ... If this assertion sounds odd to a reader familiar with the dramatic accelerations and new twists in the concluding lines of poems such as 'The Forest', 'Breasts', 'Charon's Cosmology', 'Shirt', or 'Prodigy', it will thoroughly perplex the reader of *White*, for rarely has a modern sequence of poems ended with such an apocalyptic fusion of tumult and calm – a whirlwind summoning and blending the persons, places, and things of the poet's vision. To measure their dramatic power, the two lyrics that make up 'What the White Had to Say' ought to be allowed to stand (or whirl) in the mind's eye next to the final section of Yeats's '1919' and Stevens's 'Auroras of Autumn', both of which offer similarly climactic moments of revelation and erasure.

In *White* [Simic] gives us a behind-the-scenes glimpse into what it is like to summon one's psychic forces and then watch them invade, form shapes, and displace each other. In doing so, [he] has created a poem whose ultimate immensity gives it a right to be called an epic in scale if not in length."

– Peter Schmidt, *Contemporary Literature*, 1982

RETURN TO A PLACE LIT BY A GLASS OF MILK

"... Simic's latest book ... largely seems to me to be marking time. There are many excellent poems and there is certainly no slackening in the language but what I miss is the emotional urgency one feels in the earlier poems. Simic is a poet who, like Antaeus, gains strength from the earth which nurtures the labourer and the immigrant, and as he proceeds into aerier climes some of the magic of his poetry becomes dispelled into mere games, riddles and pseudo-proverbs. At the same time his indebtedness – to Zbigniew Herbert and Vasko Popa, *inter alia* – becomes a little more obvious. His tradition is that of peasant poetry, with strong Middle European roots, and the transition to a status as an urbanized American teacher is fraught with its own peculiar perils: what began as strengths have a tendency to become mannerisms. After all, there are only so many homiletic proverbs one can rewrite, and even the ballad and child's verse forms Simic frequently uses for his variations have an inexorable law of diminishing returns."

– George Hitchcock, *Western Humanities Review*, 1974

CHARON'S COSMOLOGY

"In *Charon's Cosmology* ... Mr Simic does not write in a face-to-face confrontation with his subject and yet the effect is direct and immediate, though they are obviously of another dimension. His poems echo and re-echo in the mind, as of memories of lives, impulses and cataclysms long since buried within us ...

Mr Simic achieves his successes with the use of Symbolist and at times Surrealist techniques, but beyond the mere triumph of method lies something far more urgent for him ... He is under siege of an anxiety that expresses itself in a highly tangential manner. We all walk around with hints and allusions that flash upon us to a life we rush past in our hurry to bury ourselves in a routine way from fear. Mr Simic's fear is real for us, but his way of handling it is to reveal it to himself completely and, consequently, reveal it also to us."

– David Ignatow, *New York Times Book Review*, 1978

CLASSIC BALLROOM DANCES

"For one who vividly remembers Simic's early appearances in little magazines some fifteen years ago, it is startling to encounter him not as a new but as an established poet. But there he now stands, panting a little on that problematic ledge, mid-career, a foothold that proves sticky for some poets, slippery for others, and uncomfortable for all."

– Robert Shaw, *New Boston Review*, 1981

"There can be few serious readers of poetry who have failed to discover what this poet has to offer. The new collection ... contributes to the steady enlarging of Simic's world and canon in ways that are sometimes familiar, sometimes unexpected ...

As an artist develops and acquires increasing technical mastery, there's a danger that the means will become the end, the symbols and patterns be worshipped for their own sakes, the craft replace the vision. When this happens, the poet becomes a parodist of his or her own earlier work, and the vitality and tension begin to drain out of the poems. Simic has skirted this danger by letting recent history more and more overtly into his mythic world, cross-ventilating it, and by his experiments with form and movement. At the same time, he hasn't abandoned the terse, understated, witty mode he is master of."

– David Young, *Field*, 1981

WHITE (A NEW VERSION)

"In his willingness to rework an already successful poem, Simic shows both courage and artistic integrity. The new *White* is a carefully meditated effort to change his work constructively – not disowning what he has done, but bringing to his original insights a deepened skill and self-knowledge."

– Robert Shaw, *New Boston Review*, 1981

"Much has been made by critics of the folk influence which was so pervasive in Simic's earlier work, his preoccupation with 'preverbal, pre-conceptual consciousness', with 'childhood, folklore, eroticism, food, animals, and plants' (to quote an anonymous reviewer in *Virginia Quarterly Review*). All this seems well behind Simic now; the poems in *Austerities* are pre-eminently verbal performances, conceptual and sophisticated, allusive to a wide-range of western thought and literature ...

Austerities is a masterfully entertaining book, even at its most sombre."

– Peter Stitt, *Poetry*, 1983

SELECTED POEMS, 1963-1983

"Simic's poetry is a kind of philosophical insomnia, one wherein the present is noted and remembered but soon floats off into the formulas and imaginings of history and the unlikeliness of the future ... The imagination in these poems, which I think takes as it source *innocence*, is continually taking its first look at a first world, reacting with both awe and horror, wisdom and austerity ... Simic's work has about it a purity, an originality unmatched by many of his contemporaries."

– Liam Rector, *Hudson Review*, 1986

UNENDING BLUES

"*Unending Blues* stands not only as a fine collection of poems but as a real attempt to search for the truth that is hidden in our existence. Through his use of poetic thinking, Simic has employed a means to explore truth rather than merely repeat it. Despite the inescapable tragedy of our age, Simic also has discovered the value of the familiar to raise us above the incessant suffering inherent to any age. But once the reader peeks within its fascinating interior, it will startle, illuminate, and delight, all in the same moment of consciousness."

– Brian C. Avery, 'Unconcealed Truth: Charles Simic's *Unending Blues*', 1996

THE WORLD DOESN'T END

"A seamless fusion of wild jazz and delicate, moonstruck, European chamber music ... *The World Doesn't End* is a flawless performance by a poet at the height

110

of his powers."

– John Ash, Washington Post Book World, 1989

"Full of spunk and sass ... Simic's latest is a much-needed reprieve from the tedium that marks far too many current and 'safe' volumes of US poetry. Unreservedly recommended."

– Jim Elledge, Booklist, 1989

"A master of the absurd and the unexpected, Simic presents a collection of prose poems that will not fail to amuse and delight."

– Penny Kaganoff, Publishers Weekly, 1989

THE BOOK OF GODS AND DEVILS

"While Simic's terse, enigmatic poems have always expressed metaphysical concerns, this volume's title might suggest he is moving in an overtly religious, even visionary, direction. This expectation is only partially fulfilled by the poems. They largely represent a further exploration of styles and themes he has employed the past few years. The dualism implied by the title is played out in the way the poems balance existential dread with the possibility of hope, the way they explore both the world's 'terror and lustre'. Still, the only certainty is uncertainty. Simic creates a world of signs – 'the blue and gold Madonna in the window', a 'single ceiling fan barely turning' – that point toward a mysterious, ever-elusive meaning."

– Lawrence Rungren, Library Journal, 1990

HOTEL INSOMNIA

"A poetry of street scenes and urban gargoyles ... Simic's phantasms startle and mesmerize."

– Newsweek

"Simic writes so simply that his words fall like drops of water, but they ripple outward to evoke an ominous and numinous world."

– Washington Post Book World

"It's doubtful if there's another poet writing in America with a greater sense of clarity of image or foreboding."

— James Krusoe, *Los Angeles Times Book Review*, 1992

"Provocative, impossible to pigeonhole ... A tantalizing, beautiful fusion of visions."

— Scott Edward Anderson, *The Bloomsbury Review*, 1993

DIME-STORE ALCHEMY

"It is not surprising, given Simic's gnomic forms, that he found the boxes of Joseph Cornell — mysterious formal arrangements of synecdochic objects — peculiarly congenial. His homage to Cornell's art ... could have, as its motto, the closing sentence of one of its prose poems: 'The clarity of one's vision is a work of art.' Admirers of Cornell's constructions will be drawn to Simic's 'versions' of the boxes illustrated here.

Dime-Store Alchemy offers more, though, than poetic versions of Cornell boxes. It is a book full of art theory, full of obiter dicta on how to construct an artwork, a vehicle of reverie, an object that would enrich the imagination of the viewer and keep him company forever."

— Helen Vendler, *Parnassus*, 1991

"A beautiful book that evokes Cornell's artistic spirit."

— Arthur C. Danto, *Harper's Bazaar*, 1992

"The most sustained literary response thus far to Cornell's boxes, montages, and films ... Inclusive, free-wheeling, dramatic — a mixture of evocation and observation, as lucid and shadowy as the imagination it celebrates."

— Edward Hirsch, *New Yorker*, 1992

A WEDDING IN HELL

"Simic is a poet of quiet angst and profound scepticism. His poems reflect this in their brevity and spareness. In his newest collection, he seems to be working with a set number of images and words he uses like puzzle pieces to create a series of desolate and enigmatic poems. Some of these recurring images include a stopped clock, a dark window, a cockroach, a TV with the sound off tuned to a sex scene, and Christ in pain. Simic's blasted world lies stunned beneath the 'mad serenity' of the sky. People are destitute or, at best, uneasy, occupied with empty rituals of watchfulness undermined by apathy. These are tense and biting poems of resignation, fragmented dreams, and melancholia. Some are prayers to a muddled God half afraid of his own creations, while others reveal a bleak humour in the perversity of things, in death shadowing every glimmer of life. These poems are hard-edged and unsettling, but as you acclimate yourself to Simic's grim outlook, images of startling intensity and intelligence leap from the page like heat lightning on an oppressive night, and you nod in respectful recognition."

– Donna Seaman, *Booklist*, 1994

THE UNEMPLOYED FORTUNE-TELLER

"In this short collection of essays (some previously published in *Antaeus* and other literary reviews), Pulitzer Prize-winning poet Simic (*Hotel Insomnia*, 1992, etc.) brings off a masterfully casual beauty, whether discussing the creation of poetry and the poet's social role, praising food and the blues, or relating the travails of youth. Suspicious of all absolutist thought, the Yugoslavia-born Simic ... is a committed individualist and, like some Eastern bloc poets who have endured socialist realism, a humorous Surrealist. In deceptively discursive and casual prose, he touches on simple subjects to delve into deeper matters – for example, an autobiographical sketch chronicles his search for the meaning of human happiness in terms of favourite dishes, including Yugoslavian burek and American potato chips. Whether the subject matter is as academic as Surrealist composition, or as contemporary as the genetic engineering of his favourite fruit, the tomato, Simic gregariously mixes personal conversations with literary quotations (or, just as appositely, folk sayings and songs), and his prose can suddenly flare up into startling images: 'Words make love on the page like flies in the summer heat.' These essays' variety of approaches and subjects shows the eclectic mix of true multiculturalism, for Simic is an intellectual in the post-war model of immigrant cum exile, versed in European traditions yet enthusiastic about American culture as well. This comes into sharpest relief in his essay on murderous nationalism in Yugoslavia and his album of snapshot reminiscences of Belgrade, Chicago, and New York City. Sometimes, though, Simic's light touch fails to leave a lasting impression on the serious philosophical subjects he addresses, his selection of notebook aphorisms are hit-or-miss, and a couple of brief essays are simply culled from introductions. In one odd notebook jotting Simic projects creating a 'non-genre made up of fiction, autobiography, the essay, poetry, and of course, the joke!' – an apt description of this collection's hodgepodge charm."

– Anonymous, *Kirkus Reviews*, 1994

"The invective of his critical writings is directed against any who attempt to impose a system on the haphazard interrelations that are continually breaking down and reformulating 'reality and identity'. His targets range from deconstructionist critics (compared to 'middle class parents who do not allow their children to play in the street') to the utopian Charles Fourier who 'planned a model of perfect human society [but] was known never to laugh' ... Poetry is never figured by Simic as a solution to difficulties, but a paradigmatic means of charting them. We cherish poetry, he says, for 'its recklessness, its individualism, and its freedom'. Certainly his own work – particularly that of the last decade collected in *Frightening Toys* – is instinct with just those virtues."

– Mark Ford, *Times Literary Supplement*, 1995

FRIGHTENING TOYS

"Nearly all Simic's best poems exhibit a fidelity to the random and the partial. The concept of chance is vital to his moral and aesthetic vision ... But whereas the Surrealists sought the realm of unreason with a dedication verging on the programmatic, Simic's illogicalities are less wilfully pursued ...

Though not an ostentatiously tentative poet, Simic's 'toys' tend to provoke unnerving doubts about the most fundamental assumptions."

– Mark Ford, *Times Literary Supplement*, 1995

WALKING THE BLACK CAT

"Fanciful, mild-mannered (you're in danger of stubbing your toe on the meaning), the poems in *Walking the Black Cat* often sound like translations, or merely like translators. (Many American Surrealists seem to know the originals only in translation – why shouldn't they sound like translators?) Surrealism isn't the same in a land of Burger Heaven, Frito Banditos, and drive-in movies.

Simic's poems favour whimsical, offbeat subjects: bad TV reception, kitchen implements that talk back, a charm-school proprietor, a garden of barbed wire. Or they're about wives, playing cards, cats (a lot of cats), ghosts, any old thing, as long as it can be treated in easy-chair fashion. At worst the poems break down into a shudder of random statement and low voltage details: 'The blue trees argue with the red wind. // The white mare has a peacock for a servant.' Who would have thought even Surrealism would come down to its clichés?

Simic wasn't always so civilised ... There was a quiet menace to his early books ... the precision of nightmare made flesh. When he was young, he knew how to be savage (the arthritis set in long before he won his Pulitzer). Now he can barely be bothered to put two spirited words together. His poems exist in moral negation – there's no living emotion any more, just literary hamming (for him, the emotion was once in the seeing). His wise-guy manner is a defence against feeling, which is fine if your readers are refrigerators ..."

– William Logan, *The New Criterion*, 1996

"In each book, especially *Hotel Insomnia* (1992) and *Wedding in Hell* (1994), Simic – who has perfected a caffeinated brevity and has a gift for enigmatic images – establishes a fresh poetic lexicon and creates a new cast of characters that he sets in motion within taut metaphysical dramas. In his newest work (poems remarkable for the poignancy of their voices and terseness of their lines), he presents a coterie of sly cats, chattering birds, down-and-out men who talk to themselves, and silent, mysterious women. Each poem, each vignette, is like an old nickelodeon moving picture. They flicker silvery black-and-white as people twitch and lurch about, performing perfectly ordinary acts that are made surreal by their spasmodic movements and the inexplicable progression of light and shadow. Moody, fatalistic, ironic, and romantic, Simic conjures an alien yet familiar, dreamy yet gritty cinematographic world where city streets are a stage, mirrors reflect empty beds, and people brood about pleasure and pain, folly and beauty."

– Donna Seaman, *Book News*, 1996

LOOKING FOR TROUBLE

"Simic's strongest work is not only powerful and unsettling in its imagery, but also written against the American grain. Despite a range of American influences – from Emily Dickinson to Theodore Roethke – his swift, detached, ironic fables will inevitably strike readers as East European in character ... His short, spare, stark lyrics could slip unnoticed into the company of fellow Serbians, like Novica Tadic and Alexander Ristovic, whose poems he has translated.

... Simic continues to write impressive, arresting work; but a certain predictability of lighting, casting and scripting has reduced its dramatic effect, and his poems make a greater impact as single spies in magazines than as book-length battalions. *Looking for Trouble* contains some truly riveting poems. Yet to be repeatedly surprised in the same way is scarcely to be surprised at all, and Charles Simic is a poet who is overdue a change in direction."

– Dennis O'Driscoll, *Times Literary Supplement*, 1998

ORPHAN FACTORY

"In Simic's writing, one always hears the accent, the indelible mark of his native Serbian tongue. The accent, which in his poetry conjures the Surreal qualities of a heightened attention to language, lends to his prose a tone of curiosity and wonder – even the occasional banal phrasing is suffused with the author's rich sense of humour at the micro-comedies of modern existence. A collection of Simic's non-fiction from the past few years, the book includes selections from a memoir in progress, musings on the immigrant experience, laments for the chronic warfare in the Balkans, epigrammatic prose-poems and critical essays on poetry, painting and photography. As with his poetry, the essays are at their best when fragmentary and spontaneous ideas and images combine to link his own experiences to those of his subjects. His observations are filled with wisdom and humour, and often irreverence, as when describing the poet Robert Lowell fondling two young groupies while discussing 19th-century French poetry: 'Why wasn't I a great poet?' Simic quips. But, of course, he is, and whether you're reading *The World Doesn't End* (for which he won a Pulitzer in 1990) or *Hotel Insomnia*, or *Orphan Factory*, he is a always a pleasure."

– Anonymous, Publishers Weekly, 1999

JACKSTRAWS

"The Belgrade-born Pulitzer-winning Simic is known for his absurdist take on America's weirder tableaux (he's a sweet David Lynch), and his 13th collection is no exception. Take, for instance, 'El libro de la sexualidad': 'The pages of all the books are blank. / The late-night readers at the town library / Make no complaints about that.' Simic still has his knack for scene-setting, but one too many poems of whimsical noticings begin to grate. 'Live at Club Revolution' is strained in its cuteness: 'Are those Corinna Brown's red panties / We see flying through the dark winter trees, / Or merely a lone crow taking home / His portion of the day's roadkill?' It's hard not to admire Simic's puckish use of riffraff to support larger metaphors. But what is the ultimate significance of his numerous oddballs, the transvestites, and the women with 'flamethrower hair'? Despite the volume's kooky overload, some of Simic's pictures of casually ridiculous America still resound here: 'Hanging Christmas decorations on a string. / "She's an idealist in an undertaker's shop," / You whispered as we read the stained menu / Waiting her to turn and acknowledge us.' Poetry more akin to a compilation of wacky news stories."

– Anonymous, Kirkus Reviews, 1999

"The long sequences that end the collection – 'The Toy', 'Talking to the Ceiling' and 'Mystic Life' – are among his best: promisingly experimental in structure, crammed with bits of conversation, off-centre quips, invocations and definitions ('Memory, all-night's bedside tattoo artist') that rise above the quotidian world they alternately parody and celebrate. Simic's sly and precocious speakers are at their best when showing us 'how quiet the world gets, / When you roll your eyes back and look.'"

– Anonymous, *Publishers Weekly*, 1999

"Simic's style carries the advantage of familiarity-in-strangeness (we must 'strike a match to orient' ourselves) and the disadvantage of repetitiveness (we become oriented quickly, and then realize we aren't that dislocated). This familiarity comforts critics, who know what to expect of Simic and either praise or blame him for it (he has been heralded as the most original American poet and accused of writing translationese). Readers looking for formal ingenuity, lushness, or lyrical experimentation probably will find Simic's style disappointing. He favours the common tetrameter- and pentameter-based line, and nearly half of the sixty-two poems in the book are composed in regular stanzas of four, five, or six lines. He reveals a fondness for colloquial American speech – 'bummed out', 'lucky fellow', 'chump', 'Mr Hot-Nuts', 'fat chance' – and prefers a plain diction and flat rhythm. Exacting in word placement, Simic writes poems that demand slow reading. By stripping everything extraneous from his poems, he has arrived at the essence of the English language – 'a few words surrounded by much silence', as he has said of both Ales Debeljak's and Tadic's poetry. Because of their unadorned language, Simic's poems generally rely more on content and perspective than on music and rhythm. His way of seeing, his ability to find and illuminate details in the shadows, recommends his poems as much as his style does: 'To find clues where there are none, / That's my job now.'"

– Brian Henry, *Boston Review*, 1999

"A master of the Surreal, Simic packs his poems full of horror movies, bleak jokes, savage ironies and the things an insomniac notices on the ceiling ... A gem."

– David Lehman, *People*, 1999

"In *Jackstraws*, Simic snatches profundities from the air around him, like so many flies to some wanton boy."

– Albert Mobilio, *New York Times Book Review*, 1999

"Simic's mind is – because of his wartime youth – stocked not only with precise images of the terrifying, the incomprehensible, and the fragmented, but also with residual and free-floating clouds of feeling, which hover, ready to weep or brood, over any current experience that resonates with those earliest impressions. With the original stimuli for those inchoate feelings now forgotten or repressed, Simic seeks ceaselessly – in a constant hunger to give the clouds a reason to release their burden – for an image, a plot, a tone, anything to fasten down his troubling dreams ...

Yet there is something at work in Simic besides recollection of tragic circumstance. It is hunger for explanation; a hunger that only children really feel. Any sentient adult knows (whether admitting it or not) that life has no explanation: that truth and justice do not reign on earth, and that there is no one governing earthly events. In Simic, this adult knowledge – often explicit in the poems – keeps company with an intense wish that must have been persistent in him in childhood along with the terror he experienced: a wish that what was happening would eventually be made intelligible to him – that he could understand, as well as endure, his life.

These two motives – the search for explanation, knowing there is none; and the finding of plots or images to match the burden of feeling – have always driven Simic's poems. The results in *Jackstraws* are as brutal as they have ever been."

– Helen Vendler, *New York Review of Books*, 1999

SELECTED EARLY POEMS

"If it's permitted to speak of such a thing as a national character under our current tyranny of globalism, then there's a definite Eastern European, even Slavic, flavour to the entries in this collection. Born in Belgrade on the eve of WWII, Simic was heir to the twilit sensibilities of Mitteleuropa, which rendered everyday objects and situations with Surrealist strokes, mystical implications, and, not least, sinister overtones. It's not imprecise to refer to this demeanour as Kafkaesque in effect, if not in intent: nearly all of Simic's verses contain one or more of these disturbing elements. But unlike the Prague novelist and a postwar generation of social-realist poets, Simic's journey did not dead-end in adolescent self-absorption and life-denying seriousness. Simic made it to the US, arriving, ironically, as a teenager, quick to pick up on the American penchant for finding and expressing the humour in precisely those preposterous, though dangerous, situations. Who is Charlie Chaplin, after all, if not K with a sense of humour? An example among these early poems is 'Autumn Air', in which a man instructs his family how to assuage hunger by swallowing a good deal of air: during his demonstration, the man floats up and drifts off to sea, where he's threatened by new perils. The language here is spare, even simple, but the images are complex, challenging in the way Surrealist art defies ordinary perceptions, juxtaposing the whimsical and the frightening."

– Anonymous, *Kirkus Reviews*, 1999

A FLY IN THE SOUP

"Charles Simic is unusual in that the events of his life, both large and small, continue to interest him enormously without for a moment seeming to compete with the no less interesting but altogether different and distinctive realm of his poems. He has previously published a number of memoirs under the titles of *Wonderful Words, Silent Truth ... The Unemployed Fortune Teller ...* and *Orphan Factory ...* He has made use of details from these accounts, sometimes revising them slightly, in the course of composing *A Fly in the Soup*, an eloquent, candid, and touching account of the life he shared, off and on, with his parents in Yugoslavia and America that is, by turns, deeply moving and hilarious. ... [A] lively and heartening book."

— Anthony Hecht, *New York Review of Books*, 2001

NIGHT PICNIC

"If we have no good native Surrealists, we can at least boast of a few fine imported ones, of which Charles Simic is certainly one of the best. 'Imported', however, is the wrong term for someone who was a refugee, a DP (Displaced Person) who was born in Belgrade in 1938 and left when he was fifteen. The poetry Simic writes is not simply better than bad Surrealism; it is what we instantly recognize as a responsible mode of writing, a poetry that, for all its unexpected turns, startling juxtapositions, dream sequences, mysteries, will be found, upon careful consideration, to make a deep and striking kind of sense. It is utterly without Dali pretensions or Dada postures. It makes no appeal to the unconscious for the liberty to write nonsense. In Simic's art especially we must attune our ear to a voice usually soft-spoken, often tender, not infrequently jolly, the sort of lover of food who has been instructed in starvation. No single poem of his can be said to represent the whole range of his gifts, or the variety of his comedic sense, so often tinged with grief, or laced with that special brand of the sardonic, ironic humour characteristic of Corbière or Laforgue."

— Anthony Hecht, *New York Review of Books*, 2001

"This follow-up to the recent *Jackstraws* ... finds Simic in a relatively benign and domestic frame of mind. While his predilection for dread and his predisposition toward Surreal non sequiturs haven't entirely vanished, the poet more often turns his attention to the mundane: objects on a dresser, unmade beds, a gas station, strolling lovers ('I was warm, so I took my jacket off / And put my arm around your waist / and drew you to me'). Simic's tone is generally flat and matter-of-fact, and if evil intrudes, it barely ripples the easygoing delivery ('The devil's got his finger in every pie'). The poems are vignettes, ordinary or quirky scenes displayed at face value, vaguely inviting the reader to extend them beyond their uncertain borders via glancing references to churches, angels, and saints, convenient ciphers meant to suggest a metaphysical dimension more easily implied than articulated. Like the 'Tree of Subtleties' he describes, Simic intends to hint 'at dark secrets still to be unveiled', but blanched of sharp linguistic edges or striking images, the hints just aren't compelling enough."

— Fred Muratori, *Library Journal*, 2001

"Simic illuminates the shadow side of life in poems as perfectly formed and directed as the beam of a flashlight. He sees lovers in cemeteries after dark and ponders the secret lives of rats, crows, and worms, yet his *noir* outlook abates just enough to make room for a new strain of sardonic humour and a keen sense of the entanglement of the erotic and the doomed. Unexpected juxtapositions hit the brain like a whiff of smelling salts as he decodes the mixed messages of a street on a hot night – a thread of opera set against 'the city boiling in its bloody stew', a couple French-kissing while the homeless lie in 'dark doorways' – and considers various unlikely Christ figures, including a 'Jesus look-alike / who won a pie-eating contest in Texas'. Nabokovian in his caustic charm and sexy intelligence, Simic perceives the mythic in the mundane and pinpoints the perpetual suffering that infuses human life with both agony and bliss."

– Donna Seaman, *Booklist*, 2001

"Simic's volumes of poems – now a baker's dozen, excluding *Selected Poems* and *The World Doesn't End: Prose Poems* – are often redolent of fresh bread and other such ephemera, a notable number of which, as it happens, have involved food. Some time ago it even seemed to me that Simic was among the most gustatory of our poets ...

Simic's new book, *Night Picnic*, however, is no picnic. 'Sunday Papers' ends with 'the lamb roast [that] sat / In your outstretched hands / Smelling of garlic and rosemary', but on the whole if you're looking for delectations, colourful nature, or a moment of *dolce far niente*, you're barking down the wrong alley. These poems are what your local stationer's greeting cards become when passed through the looking glass. None of them exceeds a page – except for two sequences, in which each tiny section gets its own page – and their average length must be about sixteen lines. It is remarkable that they are that long, in view of what Simic leaves out, a list of which might begin with rhyme, meter, and other special sonic effects and extend through narrative and learned allusion to drama, to the extent that the latter involves points of view and voices other than the poet's. The diction and syntax are those of basic English – it makes perfect sense to read on the dust jacket that 'his work has appeared in translation all over the world' – and figures of any kind are sparse. The other jacket flap promises us the book will 'evoke a variety of settings and images ... [and] subjects', but in fact poem after poem deals with a small collection of closely related motifs, which include darkness, homeless people and other isolatos, vacant and run-down buildings, slaughterhouses, funeral homes, and cemeteries. In the opening poem there is 'an abandoned gas station' and near the volume's end, 'At the end of a long dark stretch' indeed, there is another one, with its 'empty office, / Its one dangling bulb.' 'We' end up waiting like Vladimir and Estragon for the absent attendant or maybe 'something / Difficult to find words for / On a late summer night without stars, / With no town or house in sight'. Along the way to this desert outpost 'Death's Little Helpers' have been legion."

– Stephen Yenser, *The Yale Review*, 2002